Travel Wisdom

Tips, Tools, and Tactics for All Travelers

May your future hold many travels gone!

Have fun — Be safe!

Hank Christen

Travel Wisdom
Tips, Tools, and Tactics for All Travelers

Lynne and Hank Christen

ɗ
Aventine Press LLC

Published by Aventine Press, LLC
2208 Cabo Bahia
Chula Vista, CA 91914, USA

www.aventinepress.com

ISBN: 1-59330-108-1
Printed in the United States of America

Travel Wisdom is dedicated to the following special people:

To our sons, Eric and Ryan Christen. You are the most important part of our lives. Thank you for all the joy you have given us. We wish for you all the happiness and passion we have enjoyed during our years together. We hope we have inspired you to see as much of our wonderful world as possible.

To Lynne's mother, Mary Nell Johnson and "Other mother" Lucille Foley. Thanks for raising me to spread my wings…and continuing to support us as we fulfill our passion for travel.

To Hank's mother, Louisa Christen. Thanks for your continuing support and encouragement in every area of our lives.

Special thanks to Marnie Tate, our best critic, proofreader, and supporter.

Special thanks to Melissa Cleary, our wonderful yoga teacher, who keeps us grounded… mentally and physically.

Special thanks to former friends and co-workers at Eastern Air Lines for the wonderful memories during our years in the sky.

About The Authors

I was ten years old when I first stepped onboard an airplane and my lifelong love affair with travel began. At age sixteen, I applied to six different airlines and received nice rejection letters telling me to wait a few years and try again. I literally counted the days until I was nineteen, the age for hiring at the time. I was finally accepted for training as a flight attendant by Eastern Air Lines in 1965.

Leaving Opp, Alabama and moving to Miami was a big step for a small town southern girl off to see the world! For the next twenty-two years I loved every minute I spent airborne. Although I later graduated from college, travel offered a far more comprehensive learning experience than long hours in the classroom. The many remarkable adventures and hundreds of intriguing people I met during my years as a flight attendant expanded my knowledge and experience, but most importantly, gave me a deep appreciation for the beauty and diversity of our world.

Hank took a different route early in life. Born and raised in Miami, he graduated from University of Florida with a degree in advertising. Eventually, his true calling won out, and he moved to Atlanta to become a firefighter...following in his father's footsteps.

We met as blind dates in 1973 and married in 1975. It didn't take long to infect Hank with my love for travel. Before we had our sons, he traveled frequently with me as I worked flights. We also took advantage of our discounted travel privileges and began our quest to see as much of the world as possible. After having our two sons, Eric and Ryan, we didn't hesitate to pack up the four of us and hit the trail. We learned first-hand the pleasures and pitfalls of traveling with a three year old or a thirteen year old. In 1986, I left the airline and Hank accepted a position as Director of Emergency Services in the Panhandle of Florida. Since that time, this has been our travel base.

Today, Hank works with Unconventional Concepts, Inc. as Director of Emergency Response Operations. He travels several times a month between his Florida office and Washington DC. With co-author, Paul Maniscalco, he has written four textbooks in the disaster management and terrorism field, including **Understanding Terrorism and Managing the Consequences**. Hank's insights and contributions in the areas of travel health and safety and business travel are an integral part of **Travel Wisdom**. After spending twelve years in banking, I've returned to the travel industry through travel writing and escorting small group trips.

Over the years, together and individually, we've have been fortunate to travel to forty-three countries and virtually every state in the United States. There is no doubt, travel is addictive. Our appetite continues to grow to see new places and re-visit old favorites. A few years ago, we discovered cruising and since that time have enjoyed fourteen cruises with five different cruise lines. We believe there is no better value for our travel dollars...as you will see in our chapter **Smooth Sailing**.

We hope you will enjoy and benefit from reading **Travel Wisdom** as much as we've enjoyed our travel experiences and writing about them. In addition to the travel tips, tools, and tactics, we especially enjoyed sharing our **Favorite Resources**, a **Few of Our Favorite Things,** and excerpts from our travel journal.

It's a wonderful world out there. We hope to meet you in our travels!

The Christens are ready to sail away on another cruise!

INTRODUCTION

September 11, 2001 changed the face of travel as it changed the face of all our lives. Over the next two years, airlines, cruise lines, hotels, tour agencies and all areas of the travel industry sought ways to enhance travel security and bring travel back to its previous status.

We believe travelers are resilient and ready to come out of their cocoons and once again enjoy the privileges and pleasures of our wonderful world. We have not curtailed our travel. Within a month after September 11, we boarded a cruise ship in New Orleans for a 12 day trip through the Panama Canal with a return flight from Acapulco. In 2003, during the war with Iraq, we flew to Venice and cruised the Mediterranean. One of our favorite ports was Istanbul, Turkey.

We are not foolhardy travelers. We are cautious travelers. We are well-prepared travelers. And, we are travelers with a love for travel that we are anxious to share.

Travel Wisdom is a book for all travelers...or those who dream about travel. It is not a destination book, but a how-to-travel guide. You may travel for the love of it...as we do. You may have to travel on business...as we do. You may be planning a family trip, but can't face the complications of traveling with a three year old or a thirteen year old. You may be single and yearn to break the barriers and travel solo. You may be a physically challenged would-be traveler. You may long to see faraway places or prefer to travel the highways and byways close to home. You may be considering a cruise to the Caribbean or the Mediterranean. Many travelers are confused and intimidated by the logistics of travel. If you want to travel smart…or travel smarter, it's all here for you in *Travel Wisdom*.

Our goals for this book are two-fold. First, we want to inspire you to turn your travel dreams into reality. Second, we want to share the practical tips, tools, and tactics we have acquired through our own travel experiences and research.

You will find detailed advice on virtually every aspect of travel, from researching and planning your trip to buying travel friendly clothes and packing less to have more. You will get answers to your questions about how to manage travel money, improve your odds for safe and healthy travel, and what to do when things go wrong. You will learn about travel etiquette. You will learn how to find and work with a travel agent, the pros and cons of group tours, and how to make your travel memories last.

Pay close attention to the **Travel Wisdom** and **Travel Experience** tip boxes throughout the text. They are our key points for each chapter. We encourage you to share your travel concerns and experiences with us. We can be reached by email at **travelwisdom@cox.net**.

It's a wonderful world! What are you waiting for?

Travel Wisdom Table of Contents

CHAPTER ONE

IT ALL BEGINS WITH A DREAM AND A PLAN

A journey of a thousand miles begins with a single step.
- Confucius

As a young girl, I spent hours perched in a mimosa tree outside my bedroom window, daydreaming about all the places I would go someday. Doing homework, I would spin the old classroom globe and pinpoint all the places I wanted to see. And, I developed my first travel plan. I would become an airline stewardess . . . that way I could see the world and get paid for it!

Over forty-five years later, I'm still twirling a globe. It's a beautiful onyx globe with all the countries inlaid in semi-precious stones. It's my travel dream globe, a special gift from Hank, to remember the wonderful places we have been and find new adventures.

Six Steps to Getting Started

1. **Dream a little.** Spin your own globe or use a good world atlas. Start a list of everywhere you dream of going. At one time my travel dream list had over 100 places on it. Today, it still has thirty-five and continues to grow as fast as it diminishes.

2. **Build a travel resource file**. Use a three-ring notebook with tabs for *Trips to Take Someday, Upcoming Trips, Travel Resources and Past Trips.* When you encounter an article that tickles your travel fancy or a website that piques your travel interest, copy it and place it in your travel file under *Trips to Take Someday.*

   For *Upcoming Trips*, include a pocket folder to hold travel documents. Get serious about upcoming trips. Research and file articles on sights to see, restaurants to try, a currency exchange calculator, a key phrases cheatsheet, and a running list of essentials to take along. File copies of your itinerary and your travel insurance certificate.

   For *Travel Resources*, create a list of travel information websites. File copies of your credit cards and passport. File an address book of key travel-related phone numbers. Last, under the heading of *Past Trips*, keep records of past itineraries, trip costs, notes on likes and dislikes, local favorites and resources.

3. **Narrow your travel choices and begin your research.** Once you decide on a destination, or maybe a couple of options, learn as much as possible about your choice/s. What are the main attractions? Make a list of "must sees." What are your options for getting there? Where will you stay? Will you take a tour or go independent with your travel plans? What will the weather be like? Are there safety and health considerations? And, of course, **how much will it cost?**

   If you're computer savvy, the Internet brings the world to your fingertips. But, there is a downside to Internet research. There is so much information that unless you know how to search; you may quickly become confused and overwhelmed. The *Favorite Resources* section of this book includes hundreds of our personal favorite travel websites and other travel resources you may find helpful.

If you don't have access to a computer, visit the library or a good bookstore and buy several books about your destination. Both Frommers and Fodors have excellent guidebooks for virtually anywhere in the world. Visit a travel agent and collect a pile of brochures. Call the local chamber of commerce or visitor's bureau at your destination and ask for information. Don't forget to organize your information in your *Travel Resource File*!

4. **If your trip includes foreign travel, get your passport early!** Allow at least ninety days before your departure . . . six months is even better. If you already have a passport, check the expiration date. Many countries won't allow you in the country if your passport expires within six months!

 As of this date, there are thirteen cities with passport agencies. In other areas, the Clerk of the Courts Office or Post Office usually has applications. You will need two 2" by 2" recent photos (available at many photo development locations), a certified copy of your birth certificate, a form of official photo identification, a completed passport application and a check for the passport fee. Check out **www.travel.state.gov** for the most current passport details. Don't put this off. With heightened worldwide security, entry documentation is much tighter and takes longer.

5. **Choose your travel companions carefully. Share research and planning.**

 While we don't have much choice about our family members (unless we opt to go solo), select your travel companions carefully. A compatible and congenial travel mate makes a trip more pleasurable. The wrong travel mate can dampen the pleasures of the best trip.

 Know each other's "hot buttons" and personal prejudices or habits that could create problems along the way. If you are a light sleeper traveling with a companion who snores like a chainsaw, you will have sleepless nights and smoldering resentment. A constant complainer can find something wrong with the best situations, and their pessimistic attitude is contagious. Know before you go!

Ask each member of your family or travel friends to come up with travel ideas. Travel research is a great way to involve older children. Ask them to "handle" some of the aspects of research and cost comparisons, encourage their buy-in to the trip, and provide a great learning tool.

6. **Get to know one or two experienced travel agents.** Although the Internet is great for gathering information and travel prices, a good travel agent is important. He or she will help you sort through the multitude of information, discover the pitfalls in your plan, come up with options when needed, help with problems that arise before and during travel, and provide the personal-service touch that Internet sources lack.

We research what we want in the way of cruises, accommodations, tours, etc. We find the best prices and give them to our travel agent to match as closely as possible. It's our travel policy to book through a local travel agent if they can come within $100.00 to $150.00 of the trip prices we are considering. Invariably they do and are able to secure additional perks not available through the Internet sources, such as shipboard credits or upgrades.

Pleasures and Pitfalls of Internet Travel Research
First, the Pleasures

The Internet is an ideal source for searching and shopping for travel ideas and resources. There are so many sources that a recent search using the word "travel" yielded 1,600,000 responses on the search engine Yahoo and 1,856,000 on the search engine Google. Way too much information! So, let's narrow the search a little by taking several types of travel and targeting how to begin to gather the best information quickly.

Destination Internet Research

Virtually every country, state and city worldwide maintains a website with information about area attractions, accommodations, restaurants, tours, parks and local weather. Many sites include maps and walking tours. We used several destination websites in California to plan an eight-day getaway through wine country. We plotted our route, selected wineries to visit, found three wonderful bed-and-breakfasts, and some great restaurants for memorable meals

Check out the websites for publishers of guide books. Our favorites are Frommers (**www.frommers.com**) and Fodors (**www.fodors.com**). Both sites offer an amazing amount of valuable destination information . . . free! Both sites offer different versions of online guidebooks that allow you to select information you are interested in, download it, and create your own custom destination plan.

Another goldmine of information is the Tourist Office Worldwide Directory (TOWD) at **www.towd.com.** This site has two pull-down menus. One menu is for foreign countries and the other is for destinations in the United States. The best thing about the site is that it is easy to use. Information on TOWD is limited to government tourism offices, convention/ visitor's bureaus and chambers of commerce. In other words, the information is non-commercially biased. There are no annoying pop-up advertisements.

When it comes to general city research, try **www.cities.com**. This website is an online guide for over four thousand cities worldwide. It's easy to use and educational even if you are an armchair traveler and just want to learn about different cities.

Cruise Internet Research

As with destination research, the Internet is a great starting point for finding the cruise of your dreams. And, as with destination research, the information available is confusing and often misleading. Success using the Internet to research cruises is improved by a narrowed focus.

The starting point, regardless of whether you are a novice cruiser or a seasoned seafarer, is to decide where you want to cruise. Then, it's important to match your travel personality and budget with the right itinerary, the right size ship (one size does not fit all!) and the right passenger demographics. A mature traveler on a Carnival Fun Ship cruise with four hundred spring breakers will not enjoy the experience. Trust us . . . we've been there!

One of our favorite websites for general cruise research and a bonanza of information is **www.cruisemates.com**. Visit this site, click on articles, and get ready for a comprehensive lesson in cruising from A to Z. Access ship reviews and ratings from previous passengers. See photos from recent cruises in an extensive photo gallery. Get your first ideas about pricing and hidden cruise costs. And, learn about specialty cruises for singles, gays/lesbians, and families. There are links to individual cruise websites that are also helpful in finding the right cruise for you.

Another great resource is **www.cruise2.com**. This is a non-profit site with information from sanitation ratings, to passenger nationalities and sample menus on most of the major cruise lines. We spend hours here!

If you don't surf the Internet, buy magazines, such as *Porthole* or *Cruise Travel.* Pick up a couple of recent books on the cruise industry. Finally, visit travel agencies. Cruise lines have extensive brochures with loads of information about their ships, itineraries, photographs and deck plans. Pick up brochures from several cruise lines that offer similar trips and compare everything.

> **Travel Wisdom: Since cruising is our travel mode of choice, you'll find much more about cruising in a later chapter. The idea now is to get you started on the research and planning track. The Internet is a great way to discover what's out there. But, when it comes to cruises, good travel agents are worth their weight in gold.**

Airline Internet Research

If you think destination and cruise research is confusing, wait until you try airline research. Airline ticket pricing is confusing, complex, and confounding. No matter where you are going, for business or pleasure, there is no single and simple source of information or ticketing.

Your best bet for airline research is to begin with individual airline websites, provided you know which airlines fly to your dream destination. While you are on the site, look at the airline's vacation packages. These packaged tours will give you an idea about pricing and tour options even if you have no interest in an airline package deal.

The site **www.airlineandairportlinks.com** is a good non-commercial website for learning what airlines service which cities. The site is easy to use and will get you pointed in the right direction if you have no earthly idea who flies where.

Plan ahead. The more flexible you are, the more shopping around you should do--and the better your chances are for finding the best deal. As a rule, the best fares are available over twenty-one days in advance.

Remember, you are just researching now, but here are some initial harsh facts of airline life to consider. Unless you want to pay full fare for an *unrestricted* ticket, a discounted fare or special fare is *non-refundable*. If you purchase a ticket six months in advance and prices go down, you will *not* be entitled to a downward adjustment. And more: if you purchase a ticket and decide to change your travel date or routing, good luck! You can count on paying a hefty *change fee* of $100.00 or more.

Travel Homework: Here's some homework for your research. (Oops . . . you didn't know there would be homework?) Check out three different airline websites and research ticket prices to the same destination on the same day. Experiment with travel a day before or a day after your original choice and see what happens. Next, research fares to the same city on the same date (and alternate dates) with several   online agency sites (Expedia, Orbitz and Travelocity). Most likely the prices will vacillate wildly. You'll quickly get the idea!

Another helpful airline research website we use frequently is **www.bestfares.com**. This site offers a great listing of last-minute deals. You can do a search of low fares by entering departure dates and destination city names. Although you can book tickets, the site is a valuable way to get a general idea of the fares and routes before you get serious about actually booking. There is also a lot of very good information about travel on this website.

What about those Internet sites you hear so much about... the ones where you name your own price? Don't get too excited! Here's how they work. You set a price you will pay for a ticket to your desired destination and then wait to see if some airline accepts your "deal." If you don't know pricing in advance, it can be a real problem to come up with a reasonable, competitive asking price.

Be aware that you must submit a charge card number *before* you submit a bid. Once you get a response and your bid is accepted, you ***automatically buy the ticket.*** No backing out. No holding the ticket while you look for another deal. You have no say about the routing. You may have to change planes or make multiple stops. You must buy a roundtrip ticket. Although you can name the day you want to travel, you cannot specify hours. You will not get frequent flyer miles. And, last but definitely not least, your ticket will be non-refundable and non-changeable. If you don't use the ticket, you are out of luck.

Why would anyone buy a ticket this way? You can sometimes get a cheaper ticket without the minimum stay requirements and without the usual fourteen to twenty-one day advance purchase requirement. (We use purchase tickets this way only for last-minute trips or in an emergency.) The majority of the time, you are best served by booking directly with the airline or through a travel agent.

Keep notes. Copy relevant information and add it to your *Travel Resource File.*

Accommodation Internet Research

Like researching airfares, begin by checking the Internet sites of leading hotel chains. Although the prices you see quoted on the Internet are a good starting point, they are not necessarily the best deal available. We initially use Internet research to check out the hotel, location, amenities, and general pricing. Then, we call the hotel direct telephone number (not the 1-800 number) and talk with reservations. When the reservations agent gives us a quote, we ask if a better discount is available. Often there is a better deal. It seems you just have to ask. Get any quote in writing!

Have no idea where you want to stay? Spend a little time browsing at some of the hotel resource sites listed in the back of this book. Don't neglect bed-and-breakfast and small boutique hotel research. We like staying at a good bed-and-breakfast. We always meet more interesting fellow travelers and enjoy unique personal experiences that large hotel chains don't offer.

Tours and Vacation Internet Research

With tour and vacation packages, your first decision during your research is whether you want to buy each part of a trip (travel, hotel, sightseeing tours, transfers, etc) separately or an all-inclusive package. There are advantages and disadvantages to both options. (See **Chapter Eleven, Pros and Cons of Group Tours.**)

Internet sites are a great way to find out about tour destinations and get details on itineraries and costs. Bears repeating: It's important to narrow your search. A search of "vacation packages" yields almost three hundred thousand responses on Yahoo. When the search is narrowed to "vacation packages to Paris" the responses drop to 35,800. Still a bit daunting! Narrow the search again to "one week vacation packages to Paris" and the responses drop to 6,300. Finally, narrowed even further to "one week cooking school vacation packages to Paris" we get 579 responses. Knowing your **travel goal** expedites your search and offers much better information than searching the world.

We recommend beginning your vacation package research with the major airline sites. Search **www.delta.com**. Click on programs and services and then on Delta vacations. At present, Delta offers about 120 vacation packages that allow the traveler to choose hotels and optional tours. The site is a good way to get an idea of package pricing. All major airlines have similar programs. No Internet? Call the 800 number for the vacation division and ask about pricing for Fly and Drive vacations. You may be shocked at the savings over booking with the regular reservations telephone number. Check and compare. Check and compare!

Another intriguing area of travel planning is specialty travel. Whether your passion is cooking, golf, yoga or cultural experiences, there is a vacation package to accommodate it. Check out **www.shawguides.com** and **www.spectrav.com**. Both of these websites include comprehensive specialty travel packages, guaranteed to get your travel juices flowing.

As with other travel offers, the pitfalls are there. Tour companies may exaggerate their claims of "best deals" and vacations extras. Note when the website was last updated. It's disappointing to get excited about "old" information that is no longer accurate and relevant. Read the fine print with a magnifying glass before you sign anything.

> **Travel Experience: Having traveled on tour packages and independent arrangements, we recommend letting the type and location of the trip play a big part in your decision. Touring wine country in California for eight days, we made all our own arrangements and thoroughly enjoyed creating our own schedule. Traveling to Bali a few years ago, we were much more comfortable (and got a much better travel deal) using a group tour package.**

Travel in the United States is relatively safe, easy to plan on your own, and not too difficult to re-coup if something goes wrong. For travel outside the country, especially to exotic destinations, we urge you to consider an escorted tour. You'll find the best deals through tour packages. There will be someone on hand to help solve problems and expedite travel arrangements. If you are a solo traveler, we strongly advise an escorted vacation package. Escorted group tours are a wonderful way to travel solo without being alone.

In summary, while the Internet offers a wealth of information and price comparisons, know its shortcomings. Heed these:

Seven Travel Traps . . . Internet and Otherwise

1. Beware of sites that require registration and fees.
Registering may not seem a problem, you simply plug in
your email address and some other information. However,
you will be flooded with email sales pitches of every nature
shortly after sharing your email address. Some websites
even have the nerve to ask for a credit card number. Don't
be too quick to share personal information or especially
pay for a "membership" for Internet information. There are
many good websites that don't require personal information
and fees up front.

2. Watch out for outdated information. Before you spend
too much time on any website, skip to the bottom of the
page and see when the site was last updated or when the
copyright was issued. If there is no date or copyright, scan
press releases, information, and offers and look for recent
dates. Call to confirm that offers are current. Avoid websites
that have no address or telephone contact number.

**3. Beware of flashing offers of travel packages. These
websites disappear as quickly as they flash on your
screen.** Rely on proven and tested travel websites.

4. Watch out for exaggerated claims. There is no Internet
patrol to police claims of "price and pledges." Don't
believe everything you see on any website. Buyer beware.
Photographs can be doctored to look much better than the
actual location. It pays to cross-check information with
more than one source.

One of the most common claims is that you have been
"selected" to receive a special vacation package. Some of
these packages require sitting through a timeshare or other
sales presentation. Other packages may include several
vacations for one "small handling fee." You pay the fee,
but when it comes time to make your vacation reservation,
there is no space available or the offer is not as represented.

When any offer is too good to be true...it is almost always **not** true.

5. **Look out for hidden fees and taxes.** The large print giveth, the small print taketh away. Add-on fees are legitimate when they are charged by governments, airports, and port authorities and customs/immigration fees. Add-on fees for service charges, handling, and agency surcharges are often a way to make an advertised price look better than it really is. Question all extra fees. While a 1% add-on may not break the deal, take it into account when making comparisons. Often if questioned, the seller quickly "waives" the fee. Wonder how much revenue comes from those who don't question?

6. **Misleading price quotes**. Most hotels quote room rates based on the room. Beware of rooms priced "per person based on double occupancy". The price you are looking at is actually *half the real price* for the room. (Note: All cruise pricing is "per person"...potentially misleading but standard practice.)

7. **Avoid offers that require *cash only* payment--usually in advance.** Never, never, never pay cash up front for travel unless you can afford to lose the money. With cash up front, if the company goes out of business or there is a problem, you have virtually no recourse. When pre-payment is made with a major credit card, the credit card company can help you recoup loses for services/purchases never received.

A travel plan is your first step. Continue on to make your dream trip a reality

CHAPTER TWO

PACKING SMART

On a long journey, even a straw weighs heavy.
-Spanish proverb

You've completed your destination research, or at least it's a work in progress. It's time to start thinking about what to take with you. Hopefully, you didn't forget to research the weather at your destination. Weather is a major component in planning your travel attire and other necessities. We've learned the hard way; you can freeze in "sunny California" in July.

The time to plan what you'll need and what you'll take is not the night before the trip. Get serious about your travel clothes, accessories and necessities at least thirty days before departure.

You are going to hear us say **"Pack Smart"** more than once. To pack smart, you need "travel-friendly stuff." Starting with travel clothes, here are some of our tried-and-true tips:

Ten Tips for Travel-Friendly Clothes for Women

1. **Begin with a three-color scheme and stick to it.** My favorite colors for travel are dark ones that don't show stains or wrinkles. I tend to go with a combination of red, black and navy with a couple of khaki or cream pieces to

break the monotony. If you don't care for red and black, try a combination of blue, grey and cream or purple, green and taupe. Become a mix 'n' match expert. It's amazing how many outfits you can get out of a minimum number of the right pieces.

2. **Stick to easy-care, no-wrinkle fabrics.** New microfiber and lightweight knits are made for travel. They look stylish. They don't wrinkle. They wash easily in a sink or shower. They dry quickly (unlike a pair of denim jeans that take days to dry in humid climates). They take up very little space in a suitcase. And, importantly, they are comfortable! If you must have your jeans, look at the new Tencel fabric jeans. They are stretchable, lightweight (pack in less than a third of the space regular jeans take) and dry quickly.

3. **Traveling to frigid areas, think layers rather than bulk.** A pair of medium-weight "long johns" worn under a pair of lightweight knit pants will keep you warmer than heavy sweat clothes that take up lots of room in your luggage. Our favorites are black silk long johns from Land's End. They feel so good and can double as pajamas!

4. **A sarong is travel necessity**. It can fill many travel needs. A sarong can be a swimsuit cover-up, a lightweight shawl, a head cover for cathedrals and shrines, a tablecloth or ground cover for picnicking. I never travel without a black sarong.

5. **When you need a warm jacket or coat, go for Gore-Tex.** Gore-Tex jackets are lightweight, amazingly warm, windproof, and waterproof. I wore one in Iceland and Greenland with temperatures well below freezing, 45 MPH winds and misting rain, and stayed warm as toast. Again, think layers rather than bulk.

6. **Don't take a two-week supply of undies on a one-week trip.** Yes, they roll up and fit in shoes and corners, but save that space for unique accessories and other small necessities. Take four or five pair of panties, a couple of

bras, and a few pair of socks/hosiery. (Easy to wash and quick to dry.)

7. **Hold the T-shirts.** Rather than filling up your luggage with T-shirts from previous trips in a myriad of colors, save the room for the ones you will buy along the way. T-shirts are usually inexpensive and a great way to add wardrobe interest as you travel. Also, when it comes to shorts, unless you are in the United States, or on a cruise ship, or at a resort, don't make shorts your daily street wear. Nothing brands you as a tourist more quickly in a foreign country. In certain countries, shorts are inappropriate. They cannot be worn in cathedrals and shrines. We watched disappointed tourists turned away at The Vatican because they were wearing shorts. Follow the old saying, "When in Rome do as the Romans do."

8. **Putting on the Ritz.** Even if you think you won't need anything dressy, be prepared. You will never go wrong with a "good little black dress." Choose a knit or washable silk in a mid-calf length. You can dress it up or down with accessories. On cruises, formal attire is needed for several nights. One elegant black dress can look totally different with a simple change of accessories.

9. **Who says a woman can never have enough shoes?** When it comes to travel, it is easy to have too many shoes! As hard as it is to cut back, shoes take up too much room in a suitcase. Leave those six pair of dyed-to-match-for-every-outfit at home. Take one very comfortable pair of walking shoes. Add a pair of flats and a pair of dress pumps. If traveling in the tropics, throw in a pair of sandals. Place a four-shoe limit on a trip of ten days or more and a three-shoe limit on trips less than one week. And, no new shoes! Travel is not the time to break in new shoes.

10. **Don't overlook scarves, belts and some great *inexpensive* accessories.** My favorite travel accessories are unique, conversation pieces of jewelry. I've got about a

couple of dozen pieces--most of which were under $10.00. Invariably, I get more compliments on inexpensive, unique pieces than on expensive jewelry.

Travel Wisdom: When traveling to other countries, especially in Asia, don't be surprised to encounter "squat toilets." These facilities are just as the name implies. It's much easier to manage these unique facilities in a skirt than in pants. Christine Columbus, travel gear, sells a personal device called a Freshette. Basically, it is a re-useable palm-sized plastic cup with a five inch detachable tube. It fits snugly over your body and allows a female to urinate standing up. Sounds weird, but works great. Ideal for times when bathroom conditions are unsanitary or primitive and for physically challenged persons. Check it out at www.christinecolumbus.com. Plan ahead.

Tips for Travel-Friendly Clothes for Men

1. **As with women travelers, think in terms of two or three basic colors to build your travel wardrobe.** Make khaki, navy and black pants in microfiber, wrinkle-free fabrics your travel wardrobe base.

2. **Look at jeans alternatives.** No matter how much you love those comfortable jeans, multiple pairs are not practical for extended travel. They take days to dry in humid weather. They take up a lot of room in a suitcase. Look at Tencel fabric jeans. They are comfortable, dry fast, and take one-third the room of regular jeans. Wear jeans with a sports coat and golf shirt enroute. (Always wear bulkier items on travel days to save packing space.) And, it's a good look for travel!

3. **Crew-neck sweaters** in a washable silk or microfiber blend look smart and are easy to roll and pack.

4. **Men's shoes--oh woe!** Women tend to take too many pairs of shoes; men's shoes just plain take up too much room. On an extended tour or cruise, you need a pair of sneakers, loafers and dress shoes. Choose pants that coordinate with one shoe color--usually cordovan. For a tuxedo, black patent is still the order of the day. (More later on how to pack shoes.)

5. **In cold climates, go for Gore-Tex.** It's lightweight, warm, windproof and waterproof. Think layers with medium-weight long johns and sweaters under a Gore-Tex jacket. Land's End silk long johns feel great and double as pajamas. They're washable and dry quickly.

6. **Underwear and socks.** Plan for four or five changes. Pack lightweights that dry fast.

7. **T-shirts and shorts** Refer to previous list for women. Same rules apply.

8. **Invest in a money belt.** With your cash divided between a wallet and a hidden money belt, you can have peace of mind that if you lose the wallet, you still have most of your travel funds.

Travel Wisdom: Dress well and you will be treated accordingly. Clothes do make the man . . . and the woman.

Travel Wisdom: Heads Up! As you purchase clothes and accessories for travel, start a file of receipts for everything you buy. Also, keep a master list of items you take along. In the event your luggage is lost, airlines do not automatically reimburse you. They want proof of what was lost and what it cost.

Choosing the Best Baggage

You've assembled a great travel wardrobe complete with all your accessories and necessities. Now it's time to choose the right type of luggage and conquer the logistics of packing.

- **Airline baggage limits are enforced and every ounce counts.** When we began writing *Travel Wisdom*, baggage limits were 70 lbs. per bag. Three months later the limit was reduced to 50 lbs. per bag. To complicate things, international airlines cut that weight restriction down to 44 lbs. per bag. The airline tab for "overweight" is hefty--as much as several hundred dollars! Overweight charges apply to each airline. If you change airlines, you pay again.

> **Travel Wisdom: Weigh your empty bag. The more your empty bag weighs, the less you can pack.**

- **We don't recommend buying expensive luggage.** Inexpensive, sturdy and serviceable bags give you as much wear as more expensive models. We have two Pierre Cardin bags that cost about $39.00 each. They are large enough for a two-week cruise with room to spare and have many features of more expensive bags. Best of all, they have survived three years of less-than-tender-loving-care by baggage handlers all over the world.

   A friend invested $275.00 in a similar-style bag about the time we bought our inexpensive ones. Her bag has not survived as well as our economy model. Expensive luggage is stolen or pilfered more often, another good reason to go inexpensive.
- **Choose a sturdy bag with wheels for both checked and carry-on bags.** Slightly recessed wheels, like those on in-line skates, hold up best. Look for a telescoping handle that catches in an "up" position. A strap at the top secures a

handbag or packages on top of the bag and makes it easier
to handle everything. Sturdy zippers are a must. Outside
zippered pockets are good for magazines and an umbrella.
Forget about the lock that comes with the bag. They're
virtually useless. Also, security may need to search your
checked bags. Secure your zippers with vinyl-lock ties that
you can clip later. They discourage and slow down baggage
pilfering. (If security must open your bag, they usually
replace tie locks.)

   Be sure to put an identification tag on both the *outside*
and *inside* of your bag. As a security precaution, use an
office address rather than your home address. Place your
destination address inside the bag on top of clothing to
facilitate tracking if the bag is lost enroute.

- **Plan ahead to distinguish your bag from other black
  pull-type bags.** Get original! We use a baggage strap
  around each bag through the handle. Straps help identify
  your bag and discourage would-be thieves from quickly
  opening your bag. Straps also prevent having the contents
  of your bag strewn far and wide if the zipper fails. We tie
  multi-colored ribbon or colored electrical tape around the
  baggage handle. Travel decals also make good identification
  markers.

   Or, if you're artistic, or have a friend who'll share
their talent, paint your bag with a dangling pocket watch, a
cluster of grapes, trailing ivy, flowers, or get really unique
and paint a dangling pink bra hanging from the outside
zipper. You won't see many of those in the baggage claim
area.

- **Departure day is drawing near. Don't wait until the
  night before to pack.** If you start packing several days
  before your trip, it's much less stressful. We designate one
  bedroom as the packing room. Our packing room has twin
  beds so we put one bag on each bed to facilitate the packing
  process. Next, place all travel items and clothing you are

taking on beds, the floor, or dresser tops. Gather everything you're taking in one place before beginning to pack. Packing is like pre-measuring and gathering ingredients for a complicated recipe. If you try to find and mix ingredients one at a time, you invariably leave something out!

> **Travel Wisdom: If you are traveling with a spouse or friend, divide your clothes and other travel items. Pack half of each person's travel items in each suitcase. If one bag is late, or never appears, you each have half of your travel items.**

> **Travel Wisdom: List everything you are packing on a couple of index cards. This cataloging system offers an instant checklist for future trips and gives you an insurance claims record if needed.**

Our Favorite Packing Tips and Tactics

Begin with your checked bag since carry-on bags can't usually be completed until the last minute.

1. **First, place a large, collapsible, lightweight, sturdy tote bag flat in the very bottom of your large suitcase.** This is your "overflow" bag for souvenirs and purchases along the way. Throw in a large black heavy-duty garbage bag folded flat. The garbage bag makes a good laundry bag to keep dirty clothes separated from clean ones.
2. **Place a couple of fabric softener sheets in the bottom of each bag.** They help keep it smelling fresh, prevent static cling in clothes, and control flyaway hair. (Rub the fabric softener over your pants/skirts to prevent static cling or your hair to prevent flyaway hair.)
3. **Place the heaviest items in the bottom of the bag.** Since

shoes (especially men's shoes) take up so much room, fill
the toes with small items and stuff 'em with socks and
underwear. Often a pair of women's shoes can be placed
inside men's shoes. Place shoes in the bottom half of the
bag so they won't shift when the bag is standing upright.
Newspaper bags work great for covering shoes to prevent
clothing becoming soiled from dirty soles.

4. **Place belts flat around the inside perimeter of the
   suitcase.**

5. **Stuff additional underwear and socks in the cracks and
   crevices around shoes.** Roll a layer of T-shirts, pajamas,
   and lightweight knits for the first layer in the bottom of
   your bag. To roll a knit item, lay it flat and face down, fold
   sleeves in, and roll tightly from the bottom up.

6. **Next, put full-sized toiletries in heavy-duty Ziploc bags
   and place on top of rolled knits.** The rolled items cushion
   the toiletries. Remove all toiletries and over-the-counter
   medications from their original boxes and place them in
   a Ziploc bag. Take sample sizes of these items rather than
   full-size on short trips. Let travel toiletries do double duty.
   For instance, shampoo makes great laundry soap for hand-
   washables. Buy individually sealed packets of items such
   as nail polish remover and spot remover. Place additional
   rolled clothing around your filled Ziploc bags to maintain
   an even packing level

7. **A hang-up toiletry bag is a travel must-have.** You have
   all your medications and personal hygiene items in one
   place. Hang the bag in the bathroom for easy accessibility.
   Our favorite travel bag is sold at Target, has three sections,
   sturdy zippers and a hidden hanger. Magellan's and other
   travel gear companies sell similar bags.

8. **Use the dry-cleaner method of folding golf shirts and
   dress or casual shirts** Button all buttons and zip zippers.
   Place the garment face down. Fold left and right sleeves
   inward at the shoulder seam straight across the back of

the shirt (one on top of the other). Fold both sides of the shirt in about three or four inches over the sleeves all the way down. Fold the body of the shirt in thirds beginning at the bottom. When you turn the shirt over the collar should be on top. Shirts folded this way can be stacked in two columns in your bag. Using a similar technique, layer several shirts or pants neatly on top of each other face down. Fold them together as one "bundle" using the method above.

9. **Now, it's time for our favorite packing technique.** The secret to packing long pants or long formals/skirts is to place them on your folded clothes base in the bag with the waistband of the pants against one of the short sides of the bag. Let the pants legs hang over the opposite side of the bag on the outside of the bag. With the bag facing you, this would be left to right. Stack a couple of pants this way. Place a few lightweight folded knits or cottons on top of the pants. Then, fold the legs in over the knits. Makes a neat bundle and prevents creasing at the pants' knees. Next, for blazers, coats or long dresses, place the collar and shoulders (buttons buttoned and sleeves folded across the coat) so they touch the far side of the bag (the long side) away from you. The bottom of the coat or dress hangs over the closest side to you. Place more folded shirts, blouses, and other items on top of the blazer and fold the bottom of the blazer over them. Another neat bundle that fights creases and maximizes space.

10. **Although some travelers swear by putting tissue paper or plastic bags between everything, we don't like either of these methods.** Plastic dry cleaner bags hold in too much moisture in humid climates. And, tissue paper is more trouble than it is worth.

11. **Roll neckties and scarves and place in corners or coat pockets.**

12. **Place each necklace through a plastic straw to prevent tangling. Stick pierced earrings through a thin piece of cardboard and put backs on.** Place jewelry in a large or medium Ziploc bag. (Remember! Leave your heirlooms at home and take unique conversation pieces you can afford to lose.)

13. **It's more damaging to underpack than to overpack.** When you underpack, clothes shift and wrinkle more. If by some wild chance your bag is not full, use bubble wrap or an old towel to fill the space. Ditch the towel as you add purchases that fill the bag.

14. **Before you close the bag, place a detailed copy of your itinerary (include your destination address) on top of your clothes.** This itinerary helps locate you at your subsequent destinations if your bag is lost or delayed. Take a photograph of your bag to assist in identification.

15. **When you finish packing, do a baggage test.** Practice handling your baggage. Be sure you can lift it on and off baggage conveyers. Weigh your bag to be sure it's not overweight while there is still time to discard some items.

Becoming a Carry-On Traveler

Yes, it can be done. One of the most important aspects of becoming a smart traveler is learning how to travel light. Although this may be perceived as a sexist remark, this is normally a more difficult task for women than for men.

I Can't Carry-on Excuses

 # One: "I might need this." Unless you are traveling to a third world country with minimal resources, there are few items you cannot obtain at your destination. Yes, it is comforting and convenient to have your travel necessities and luxuries at hand. Be realistic. Take travel sizes of luxury must-haves…even if you have to downsize them yourself.

#Two: "I must have something new to wear everyday." Why? If you practice the mix-and-match theory of travel wear, you should be able to get three times the wear out of your individual pieces and never wear the "same outfit twice."

#Three: "I need *clean* clothes everyday." Good, so do I. New fabrics, such as Tencel and other microfibers, can easily be washed in the sink or shower at night and be fresh and dry in the morning. Dark colors don't show stains. Travel packets of Woolite or shampoo make "sink" laundry a breeze.

#Four: "What about space for the things I buy along the way?" Pack a collapsible tote bag in the bottom of your carry-on. Ship purchases home. Buy a "cheap" bag to check on the way home if shopping purchases become too tempting.

Basics for Becoming a Carry-on Pro . . .

- **Have the right travel wardrobe**. You can pack an amazing amount of the *right* clothes in a carry-on bag. New-generation fabrics such as Tencel, lightweight microfibers, knits and silks are made for travel. Need ideas? Order catalogs from TravelSmith, Magellan's, and Christine Columbus and get a great education in travel wear, including mix-and-match color ideas.

Personal Experience: I swear by two and three piece outfits by Rafael under the label, Pleat Pleat. Although they are bold prints, they mix well with solids. They are incredibly lightweight. They are washable and don't wrinkle. They are comfortable. They are reasonably priced, but chic.

- **Choose double-duty wear.** For example, a long T-shirt or sarong becomes a bathrobe. All of your tops match all of your bottoms.
- **Purchase a compact toiletries bag and travel sizes of all products.** Remove over-the-counter products from boxes and downsize larger products that don't come in travel sizes yourself. Again, look for double-duty products. Shampoo makes great laundry soap for washables in the sink or shower.
- **Wear your bulkiest clothes and shoes.** If you need them at your destination, wear a raincoat or jacket on the flight, even if it's 90 degrees and sunny outside. Save packing space!
- **Airlines currently allow travelers one carry-on under 45 linear inches and one smaller personal item.** Personal items are purses, briefcases, cameras or diaper bags. Choose the largest personal item possible, as long as it's smaller than your carry-on and looks like a purse or briefcase. Place a smaller handbag in the larger one. Put toiletries and make-up in this bag. Leave room for your snacks and in-flight comforts. Cram a change of clothing (or at least underwear) in a Ziploc bag in this bag.
- **Rarely happens, but overhead bins could be full when you board. (See airline seat selection in Chapter Thirteen).** In this case, you may have to check your carry-on bag. That's a good reason to have your absolute essentials in the personal bag. Be sure it will fit under a seat!

Personal Experience: We traveled to Hong Kong for eight days with only a carry-on and a personal bag each. We had everything we needed and never wore the same thing twice. With the incredible shopping opportunities in Hong Kong, needless to say we did not come home with only our carry-on bags. We solved our extra packing dilemma by purchasing an inexpensive large bag ($18.00) to check. We put all our dirty clothes and non-essentials in the checked bag and packed our new purchases and essentials in the original carry-ons. This made clearing customs easier since everything to declare was in the two carry-on bags.

Once you become a seasoned carry-on traveler, you will enjoy the freedom of being able to catch an earlier flight when the opportunity arises. You will breeze through the terminal on arrival, past the passengers waiting nervously for their checked baggage. And you will have the smug pleasure of being one of the elite--the envied professional traveler not anchored down by luggage filled with clothing and items you will not need.

Travel Wisdom: See checklists in Travel Resources for more ideas.

CHAPTER THREE

CHOOSING A TRAVEL AGENT

The amount of travel information available is overwhelming. The Internet returns hundreds, thousands or even millions of travel options. Magazines, newspapers, television travel shows and guidebooks add to the confusion. You may easily "be your own travel agent" for short, simple trips. However, when an itinerary is complicated (with multiple travelers and multiple destinations), a professional travel agent is invaluable. In spite of the resources online, travel agents are not obsolete.

According to statistics from the American Society of Travel Agents, travel agents are still the leading distributors of travel services. Travel agents book 75% of all travel, 30% of all hotel reservations, and 95% of all cruises.

Travel Agents Provide Services

- **Sorting through the information**. When the agent knows you and understands your needs, they can facilitate reviewing your travel options and choices.
- **Researching the most competitive travel deals.** If you call an airline directly, they will never tell you that a

competitor has a flight on the same day at one-third of their cost. A travel agent is your travel advocate.

- **Accessing and analyzing special travel promotions.**
- **Helping you decipher the small print, such as cancellations, penalties, and restrictions.**
- **Offering added travel perks and benefits, such as recommendations on where to shop, what sights to see, and where to eat.**
- **Getting problems resolved**. Travel agents have more clout than individual travelers when it comes to buying power and problem-solving savvy.
- **Finding last-minute travel opportunities.**

It's equally important to understand what a travel agent *cannot* do for you. Travel agents cannot guarantee you a perfect trip. They cannot "double-book" you on different flights or with multiple airlines so you have back-ups. They cannot guarantee that your flights will be on time or that a cruise ship or tour group will wait for you. Although they negotiate with airlines and hotels, they cannot prevent travel problems and their consequences. It is unrealistic to expect everything to be perfect and to hold them to unrealistic standards. Finally, they can be your advocate when there are travel problems or emergencies, but they are *not* ultimately responsible for missed flights, lost bags and unavoidable travel disappointments.

Finding a Good Travel Agent

Finding a good travel agent is like finding a good lawyer or realtor. It is important to choose an agent who understands your travel style and is interested in establishing a long-term relationship with you . . . not just making a quick sale.

Ask friends and associates who travel frequently which agency they use. Look under travel agencies in the local telephone book. Call or visit the agencies on your "prospect" list. The way the agency answers the telephone and responds to your initial inquiry will give you a good idea how they approach customer service. Asking some basic questions can also help narrow your choices:

- What professional training do you/your agents have?
- What type of travel do you specialize in?
- Are you a member of the American Society of Travel Agents (ASTA) or other trade associations?
- What services do you provide and what services do you charge for?
- Do you have a 24-hour help-line for travel problems/needs?
- Do you have a brochure or newsletter from your agency?

If the agent is too busy to respond to your telephone inquiries, make an appointment to visit the agency. If the agent doesn't welcome your visit and is not interested in spending the time to learn about your travel preferences and concerns, find another agent who is.

Helping Your Travel Agent Help You

Know where you want to go and have a realistic idea of how much you can afford to spend. Begin by discussing the purpose of your travel--business, pleasure, education, visit family, seek medical care, etc. Do your homework. Collect cruise, tour or other travel advertisements from newspapers and magazines. Search travel websites for travel packages, tours and airfares. It helps to have some idea about travel costs so that you don't waste your time and the agent's time planning a trip that is too costly or doesn't meet your needs.

Discuss how many people are traveling with you and any special requirements they may have, such as disabilities, single supplements, or minor children. If cost is your primary consideration, make sure the agent understands this and offers cost-saving options.

**Travel Wisdom: Keep in mind that you get what
you pay for. Cheapest is not always the way to go.**

A good travel agent works with you to determine when to
cut corners and when to stretch your budget a bit. Be open-
minded to the agent's suggestions and receptive to alternative
ideas. Discuss offers you see advertised or on the Internet with
your agent and rely on them to check out the validity of the
offer and give you a comparison.

**Travel Experience: We frequently uncover offers
on the Internet and give our agent the opportunity
to match them. If she is within $100.00 or so of the
price, we use her services because we know she will
stand behind her offer and go the "extra mile" in
customer service.**

Local Versus Online Travel Agencies

The Internet offers an abundance of travel agencies. It is
relatively easy to shop for airplane tickets, hotels, cruises, and
tours online. Some of these booking sites are very good and
will save you a lot of money. Others are not so good. Some are
dishonest and their offers are actually travel scams. Do your
homework before you click and buy. Here are some ways to
find reputable online agencies:

- **Research a hypothetical trip**. Pick a destination and
  research various ways of getting there, accommodations,
  sightseeing, and other travel options.
- **Create a flow chart of options and costs.**

- **Note which websites offer alternatives versus giving you only one choice.**
- **Subscribe to online newsletters or mail offerings from several agencies and see how they compare.**
- **Review the agency's contact information.** If there is not a 1-800 customer service telephone number, forget that site. If there is a 1-800 number, test it. Call customer service and see how knowledgeable and helpful the representative is. Inquire about 24-hour assistance in the event of problems or last-minute needs.
- **Compare, compare and compare** before you make the decision to buy.
- **Check out the online agency with the Better Business Bureau and travel trade associations such as ASTA or IATA.**

Regardless of whether you select a local travel agency or an online travel agency, keep these final thoughts in mind:

1. **Don't rely on verbal agreements and promises.** Get everything in writing.
2. **Read everything carefully . . . especially the fine print.** Be sure you understand cancellation policies and all restrictions and limitations.
3. **Charge all travel on a credit card.** If the agency doesn't accept credit cards go elsewhere.
4. **Don't be pressured into making hasty travel decisions.**
5. **If you are promised extra amenities,** such as upgrades or complimentary nights or meals, get these promises in writing.

On a final note, be good to your travel agent. When they go "above and beyond" for you, let them know you appreciate their services. Refer business to them. Bring them a token of appreciation from your trip. Send a thank-you note. Travel agents, like anyone who works with the general public, encounter all types of clients. Most clients are pleasant, courteous and reasonable . . . a few are unreasonable, unrealistic and unpleasant. **Who do you think gets the best service?**

CHAPTER FOUR

THE DOLLARS & SENSE OF TRAVEL

This chapter is not about how much travel will cost you. Travel costs are determined by how you travel, length of travel, where you stay, what you eat, and so forth. Suffice it to say, you will spend more than you initially think.

This chapter is about learning how to get the most for your travel dollars and protect your travel funds. As a banker for over ten years, I was often surprised at how misinformed people were when it came to travel finances. So let's begin by taking a look at how, when and where to get your travel money.

What Kind of Money to Take

Whether you are traveling in the U.S. or abroad, your travel dollar options are very similar. Travel funds may be in the form of cash, travelers checks, ATM/debit cards, and credit cards. We recommend a combination of all four . . . especially for extended trips or trips outside of the U.S.

Cash Travel Funds

Always plan to carry a cushion of cash. That said, carrying too much cash is dangerous. Invest in a good money belt or neck pouch before you travel . . . regardless of whether you are traveling in the United States or abroad. You are in as much danger of being mugged in a U.S. city as in Barcelona, Bogota or Beijing.

A money belt is not exactly as the name implies. It is not a belt, with secret zippers, worn to hold your pants up. A money belt or neck pouch is a small leather or nylon pouch that connects around your waist or neck *under* your clothing. Don't confuse a money belt with a "fanny pack." A fanny pack is one of the most dangerous ways to carry travel funds. Thieves can easily slit the straps or top of the bag and disappear with your money before you know it is missing. You can order a good money belt from Magellan's for under $10.00.

Keep your essential documents, credit cards, and majority of cash in the money belt. Keep a minimal amount of cash for small purchases in your handbag or pockets. Don't keep more cash easily accessible than you can afford to lose. When it is necessary to get a credit card or cash from your money belt, be discreet. Don't make a production of counting off bills from a roll or flipping through multiple credit cards to find the right one.

Some travelers get foreign currency before leaving the U.S. We don't. Foreign currency is expensive to purchase in the United States. Your local bank does not keep it "in stock." It has to be ordered in advance and for a fee. If you are arriving at an odd hour and need the security of having a few dollars in local currency, go ahead and pre-purchase $50–$100 in foreign currency to tide you over. Don't get all your money in advance this way!

Travel Wisdom: Be sure to exchange foreign currency back to U.S. currency before leaving the country you are visiting. Better yet, spend it in the airport. Avoid the inconvenience of having to exchange it and pay another fee. Also, foreign coins are generally worthless outside their own country. Spend them, give them away, or keep them for souvenirs. Creative hint: Foreign coins look great glued to a photo frame to showcase a travel photo.

Travelers Checks

Travelers check usage has declined since the introduction of ATM and debit cards. However, they are still a viable and relatively convenient and safe form of travel funds. We almost always get some "emergency" travel money in the form of American Express Travelers Checks. We rarely use them during the trip and end up depositing them back to our bank account when we get home. We keep them separate from our credit cards and cash as a back up. If lost or stolen, they can be replaced. (Caution: Do not keep your receipt with the travelers checks. Have your travel companion carry the receipt for your checks and vice versa. If you are traveling alone, keep the receipt in a separate bag.)

If you do opt for using travelers checks as your primary travel funds, you will get the best exchange rate at American Express offices, banks or post offices. Except in an emergency, avoid the exchange bureaus you see on every corner in tourist shopping areas. They almost always have the poorest rate of exchange. The posted rates at exchange bureaus are misleading and you may be charged extra handling fees or per item for the transaction.

ATM/Debit Cards

Whether you are traveling in the United States or abroad, ATM machines are a convenient and easily accessible source of cash. Cash withdrawals from an ATM machine are at wholesale bank rate. Even with the usage fee; you typically get a better rate of exchange. There are literally thousands of automatic teller machines linked through systems like Cirrus, Star and Visa. (Caution: Know what systems your ATM card is valid with before leaving the country. Look for ATMs that use one of your systems.)

On a trip to Bali we arrived at midnight with no local currency. Airport ATM machines supplied our group with

Indonesian rupiah. We felt wealthy getting two million rupiah-
-the equivalent of about $234 in U.S. currency.

Cautions for ATM Usage

* Activate and try out a new ATM card *before* leaving on
  your trip. An ATM card can only be activated by doing a
  balance inquiry at an ATM machine or from your home
  telephone number. Don't wait until you need cash before
  activating the card. Activation usually takes 24 hours to be
  effective.
* Memorize your PIN (personal identification number). Do
  not write it on the card or in your checkbook.
* Notify the card company that you will be traveling abroad.
* If your PIN is composed of letters, look on the telephone
  pad and convert the letters to numbers (memorize the
  numbers) before leaving the country. This is not about
  getting a "new" ATM PIN . . . it's your same one, just
  in a different format. It's hard to mentally convert letters
  to numbers standing in front of an ATM that only uses
  numbered codes.
* Check and possibly increase your daily withdrawal limit.
  Most ATM cards are capped with a $300 daily limit. You
  can request, in writing, that the limit be increased. Plan
  ahead. You can't do this by telephone after leaving the
  country.
* Guard your PIN during usage. Shield the keypad with your
  other hand. Don't use a machine when there is someone
  loitering nearby.
* Be sure to take your receipt and hang on to it. You will need
  to verify the correct transactions to your account when you
  return home.

As with all forms of travel funds, do not depend on *just* an
ATM card for your travel dollars. ATM systems can be "down"
or your card's magnetic strip can be damaged and your access

to cash may be cut off. Avoid using eel skin wallets or putting
your card near magnetic surfaces.

Credit & Debit Card Travel Funds

What's the difference? A credit card is a form of credit .
. . just as it says. When you use a credit card for purchases
or cash advances, you will receive your regular monthly
statement to pay in full or installments. A debit card does just
what it says. It debits your checking account for the amount
of the transaction. Both cards have advantages for travel. The
most widely accepted credit cards are Visa and MasterCard;
although American Express is growing in popularity. Using
a credit card, like using an ATM card, offers the benefit of a
wholesale bank exchange rate. Many cards also offer "perks"
such as cash rebates or airline mileage. On a cruise to Europe,
we charged our ticket and got an additional 4800 miles in
addition to our actual air miles for our flight.

Finally, when you use a credit card for purchases, you get
some form of purchase protection. Never pay for a purchase
to be shipped without using a credit card. Pay cash and fail to
receive the goods . . . you are out of luck. Use a credit card
for purchase and you have at least some "insurance." Check
with your card company before leaving to determine what
travel benefits are offered.

Since most debit cards are processed through the Visa or
MasterCard system, it is as easy to use them for purchases as
it is to use a charge card. That said, they do not offer the same
purchase protection or benefits as a major credit card. They
are essentially the same as paying cash.

Even if you are opposed to using credit cards on a daily
basis, we strongly recommend that you take at least one major
credit card for travel. If you have a medical emergency or
another type of emergency, a credit card can be a lifesaver!

> **Travel Wisdom: If traveling with a companion, each of you should take a different credit card. If one card is lost and you must cancel it, you still have a back-up card.**

> **Travel Wisdom: Make a copy of both sides of your ATM and credits cards before you leave and keep the copy separate from your cards. Leave a copy of all credit cards you take at home with friends or family. In the event of loss or theft, you can quickly cancel the cards.**

> **Travel Wisdom: Notify your credit card companies in advance where you will be traveling. Most companies have security procedures that call for automatically canceling a credit card if "strange" purchases start appearing—especially from foreign countries.**

The well-prepared traveler doesn't depend on any one method of travel funds. A combination of the above financial resources offers you the peace of mind of knowing that your travel needs, both for pleasure purchases and in an emergency, are covered.

Travel Insurance. Don't Leave Home Without It

When was the last time you knew in advance you were going to get sick . . . or an immediate family member would have an emergency illness? When was the last time you knew in advance a hurricane or other disaster would close the airport and stop all travel? Do you know for sure your current insurance will cover you if you have to be medically evacuated from another country in order to get proper treatment? Get the idea?

Life is full of surprises and uncertainties. We never know when a medical emergency or disaster will occur. We've said it before: When it comes to travel, be prepared! And, travel insurance, even though we hate to pay it, is an important part of being prepared.

Research insurance you already have. What does it cover and not cover during travel? For instance, some medical policies cover medical treatment and medical emergency evacuation out of the country, most do not.

Travel Wisdom: Many seniors are not aware that Medicare does *not* cover you outside the United States.

Some homeowner's policies offer protection for baggage loss or theft and some credit card providers include an accidental death benefit if you charge your trip on their card. Check on existing coverage you have from these sources, but don't be surprised if it's not much! We strongly recommend that you protect your travel investment and your wellbeing by purchasing travel insurance.

What Is Travel Insurance?

There are several different types of travel insurance ranging from trip cancellation to full medical coverage, including medical evacuation. Usually one comprehensive policy covers all aspects of travel, but you have to know what you need and be thorough in your research before you purchase any policy.

A medical travel insurance policy covers you in the event of illness or injury during your trip. You will be reimbursed for reasonable medical expenses. Consider the area you are traveling in. In remote areas of developing countries, medical care is limited at best and you will need medical evacuation to get adequate care. Medical evacuation is very costly; ranging from $35,000 to $50,000 on average.

Medical travel insurance provides an emergency telephone number accessible from anywhere in the world to assist you in locating an English-speaking physician. This policy also covers returning your remains to your home in the event of death.

> **Travel Wisdom: We have a friend who experienced illness with a medical evacuation and another acquaintance whose spouse passed away unexpectedly on a trip to Italy. Both couples had medical travel coverage to assist them in this time of great stress and need.**

Trip cancellation/interruption insurance offers protection in the event something unexpected forces you to cancel or interrupt your trip. Most policies cover cancellation/interruption due to illness or death of you and your immediate family or your travel companion, even if not related. You are also covered if your travel agent, tour company, or cruise line defaults. And, coverage includes baggage loss and delay protection.

Prior to the terrorist attack of September 11, most policies did not cover acts of war or terrorism or cancellation due to threat of terrorism. Recently, some companies are including a rider for this type of coverage. Finally, most airlines either restrict or prohibit changes to travel tickets without significant penalties. Tickets purchased at auctions and through some consolidators cannot be changed or refunded. Some travel cancellation/interruption policies reimburse part of the cost of changing your ticket.

Be aware that the majority of travel insurance policies exclude pre-existing medical conditions. If you or a family member has a chronic medical condition, check any proposed policy carefully to ensure you will be covered. Most waivers of pre-existing conditions require the purchase of the insurance within seven to ten days of booking your trip. Plan ahead!

Costs of travel insurance vary with the coverage provided. "Least expensive" is **not** the only criterion you should use to select a policy. Policies are priced by the type of coverage you require, the length of your trip, cost of your trip and travelers' ages.

> **Travel Wisdom: If you travel frequently for business or pleasure, it would be worthwhile to consider an annual travel protection policy. Fees normally average $299.00 per person, significantly less than insuring multiple trips. The medical coverage is more comprehensive than individual trip policies.**

MedJet

When it comes to travel insurance, there is one company we feel deserves special mention. If you travel frequently, you should consider additional insurance from Med Jet. Med Jet is an air medical provider based out of Alabama. They do not offer traditional travel medical insurance. They offer an annual membership for prepaid air ambulance transportation. Their service provides frequent travelers with worldwide evacuation and repatriation air ambulance benefits designed to get them back to their hometown from any destination more then 150 miles from home.

At the current time, a one-year contract with Med Jet is approximately $195 for individuals and $275 for families. For this fee you get medical transportation back to your hometown hospital from any destination more than 150 miles from your home base. There are no pre-existing conditions clauses, and no maximum dollar limits. Transportation is not just to the nearest medical facility, but to the hospital of your choice. No additional doctor's approval/requests are required.

Of course, there are restrictions, but for frequent business or pleasure travelers, this service could be a lifesaver. Benefits exceed traditional travel insurance benefits for air evacuation. For more information, contact MedJet at **www.medjet.com** or 800-356-2161.

> **Travel Wisdom: Purchase insurance from an independent company rather than through your tour operator or cruise line. If the operator or cruise line defaults your insurance may be invalid.**

One of the most comprehensive websites for researching travel insurance is **www.worldtravelcenter.com.** The site offers comparisons of all types of travel policies from a multitude of companies. Spend some time studying your options and choose well.

> **Travel Wisdom: One final caution, as with all travel documents and agreements, read all policy information carefully before you purchase— especially the fine print.**

Shopping Savvy

On a more pleasurable note when it comes to travel dollars and sense, shopping plays a significant role in the enjoyment and the cost of your trip. Budget your shopping dollars, as you do your food, lodging, and transportation; however, expect to spend more than planned. From giant malls to quaint markets, travel offers an array of shopping experiences.

We love to wander through local markets, discovering treasures to add to our travel memorabilia collection. I always seek out one unique piece of inexpensive jewelry. Hank is a maritime collector and gravitates toward anything nautical. We also always purchase some local handicraft as an ornament for our Christmas memory tree and an inexpensive poster or artwork for our "garage travel art wall."

Research Shopping as You Prepare for Your Trip.

- **Research guidebooks and websites** to get an idea about local shopping opportunities awaiting you.
- **Print or copy maps** and highlight intriguing stores and markets.
- **Print a currency exchange cheatsheet** from **www.oanda.com** .Wait until a day or so before the trip, so those exchange rates are current.
- **Make sure your credit cards are not near expiration.** Notify the card provider of the countries where you'll be using your credit card.
- **Pre-print mailing address labels to ship merchandise home if you plan to do serious shopping.** (Remember you'll have a collapsible bag if you follow our packing checklist.)
- **Be careful of telling friends and family about all the great bargains where you're going.** You may end up with a long shopping list for others.

Sharpen Your Bargaining Skills

In local markets and bazaars in many parts of the world, bargaining is an integral part of your shopping experience. Some travelers enjoy bargaining; others find it uncomfortable. (I love it. Hank hates it, but is getting better!)

Do's & Don'ts of Successful Bargaining

- **Do ask about local bargaining protocol.** Check with the cruise director or hotel concierge.
- **Do a price patrol.** Note prices for items you are interested

in stores at home or on the Internet. Compare prices at several local shops before buying. Know your prices.

- **Don't be coerced by an aggressive shopkeeper**. They are experienced and talented hagglers. Don't let them intimidate you.
- **Don't touch or pick up an item unless you are interested in it**. The seller will immediately begin negotiations and continue to hassle you, making it difficult to enjoy shopping.
- **Don't ask the price of an item you want right away.** Try to act indifferent about it. You "may" be interested if the price is right.
- **Do begin bargaining at 50% of the asking price.** Expect to end up paying about 60% to 80% of the original asking price. Look for theatrics from the seller.
- **Do try to shop early.** In many markets, sellers feel early sales bring luck the rest of the day. They are more willing to give in to a lower price to "get the luck."
- **Do decide what you are willing to pay and stick to it.** State firmly "that's all I can spend."
- **Don't haggle over pennies.** When negotiations reach that point, give in. Consider the economic conditions where you are. A few cents means much more to a poor economy than to your shopping experience. Expect to get "taken" occasionally. It's all part of the experience and not catastrophic if the amount is small. Makes a good travel story, if you admit to it!
- **Do act knowledgeable about prices and exchange rates.** Use your currency cheatsheet and don't get bamboozled by manipulated exchange rates. A current favorite ploy is for merchants to whip out a calculator and punch in the asking price acting like they have put great thought in calculations. We have experienced this in Italy, Turkey, Hong Kong,

and Mexico. Ask for the calculator and enter your own "calculation."

- **Do discuss payment method and shipping methods in advance.** Credit card purchases may be a little higher. The merchant has to pay to accept credit cards. Ask about additional cash discounts. Get the exact cost of shipping. Produce your label and insist on watching the package wrapped and labeled for mailing.
- **Don't get flashy with your money.** Be discreet in paying with cash.
- **Do be willing to walk away if you can't reach a price agreement.** Don't be rushed. The seller will probably follow you and give in. If the seller gets pushy or disagreeable, leave immediately.

Travel Wisdom: When shipping, pay only by credit card. Watch credit transactions carefully. Indicate whether funds are in local and U.S. currency. Take the carbon with your receipt. Keep the receipt in case of discrepancy or dispute. Jot the exchange rate on the receipt. If there is a discrepancy, contact your credit card provider and file a claim. They will handle it from there.

Do take along some small gifts. Items such as inexpensive sunglasses, bandannas, and ballpoint pens are sought after in many countries. Visit the Dollar Store and stock up before your trip. Enjoy the pleasure, goodwill and memories that small gifts bring.

Travel Experience: Hank's Favorite Bargaining Story-When we were in Bali, Hank was negotiating with an assertive young man for an antique ship compass. Toward the end, the seller commented on Hank's sunglasses ($3.00 at Wal-Mart). Hank said, "Okay I'll throw the sunglasses in as part of the payment." The seller was ecstatic. Putting them on, he strutted around, saying, "Now I look like American movie star." We didn't really save any money on the purchase, but it made the whole transaction more memorable and more fun.

Travel Experience: Lynne's Favorite Bargaining Story-My favorite bargaining purchase was in Cozumel, Mexico. It is a large, silver (look for the .925 stamp for authenticity) Aztec calendar medallion with a silver choker necklace. The price started at $60.00 and after much good-natured bargaining on seller's part and mine, I paid $25.00 for it. The seller told Hank that I "was a tough lady and he felt sorry for him." Since that purchase, we have been back to the market and that store three times and bargained for several other unique pieces. The seller and I are "old friends."

Have fun shopping and bargaining. Enjoy your purchases and the memories they give you!

CHAPTER FIVE

TRAVEL HEALTH AND SAFETY

It's important to enjoy your trip safely and in good health, whether you travel for business, adventure, or pleasure. No one says, "I got sick and mugged after the hotel fire; other than that, it was a good trip."

It's a myth that travel is risky or dangerous. In October of 2002, terrorists assaulted a Russian theater and Americans were thinking, "Thank goodness I wasn't in Moscow attending the theater." At the same time, Russians were thinking, "I'm glad I'm not in the United States where a sniper is shooting everybody."

Some of your greatest travel risks begin at home. People don't worry about safety in America, but become concerned when traveling abroad. Unfortunately, you have a greater chance of being a non-war gun violence victim in the United States than in any other country. Statistics also show that 80% of accidents happen in the home. The point: Go ahead and travel, but remember that travel safety begins before you leave.

The LACES Principle

Travel safety involves some basic rules. If you forget everything else, but remember the basics, you'll be a safe and healthy traveler.

LACES stands for Lookout, Awareness, Communication, Escape, and Safety. These principles were originally developed by wildland firefighters after analysis of multiple firefighter injuries or death events revealed at least one (or more) of the LACES principles were violated in each case. The LACES principle applies to travel safety, so let's look at each element in the LACES acronym. (Think about shoelaces as a reminder.)

Lookout **means "looking out" for your companions.** Lookout is a partner seeing and/or perceiving threatening situations. For example, pickpockets may create a diversion by jostling your spouse while a cohort steals his or her wallet. Your spouse may not sense the threat, but you're on the lookout.

Awareness **is having a "situational awareness" of your surroundings (especially if you're alone without a lookout).** Awareness is "big picture" instead of "narrow focus." Continuously look around and appraise your surroundings. Unaware pre-occupied tourists make easy targets. When you arrive, survey the neighborhood. Ask what areas are safe. On the street, keep looking around and behind you. Most importantly, trust your instincts. When hairs stand up on the back of your neck, a primitive warning system is telling you something. Read *The Gift of Fear* by Gavin de Becker.

If you are drunk, stoned or high, you can't maintain awareness. There's no moralizing here . . . if you indulge, be careful where you do it. Being drunk on a strange street greatly reduces your ability to perceive and react to threatening events.

Communication **is sharing information with those around you.** Give a written itinerary to friends or family (it's like filing a flight plan) before you set sail. If you are in a country for more than two weeks, give your itinerary and contact information to the American embassy or consulate. They will contact you if travel or evacuation warnings are

issued. Communication also means transmitting warnings to
your companions and calling emergency agencies.

Escape **means planning an exit route.** Think about which
direction you'll take to get to safety. (We'll cover escaping
from airplanes, fires, ships and trains later.). Always think,
"Where's an exit or escape route?"

Safety **means finding a safe zone.** Safety is exiting a
building in a fire or attack, or running to a firehouse, police
station, or lighted area. Safety is the lifeboat station on a ship
or the emergency slide on an airplane. A safe zone is the end
of an escape route or a muster site. Plan a location where you
and your partner or companions can regroup if your normal
area becomes dangerous. Lynne and I always pick a park
or another hotel within walking distance. If we're apart and
something happens at the hotel, we look for each other at the
muster site. On cruise ships we plan to meet at our lifeboat
station, and plan an alternate site (for example the bow on the
lifeboat deck) if our assigned station is threatened.

> **Personal Experience: In September 2001, when
> Hank's medical disaster team was at the World Trade
> Center, there were warnings about another attack.
> They selected a park near New York City Hall as a
> muster site to regroup and count heads. Fortunately,
> it wasn't necessary.**

> **Travel Wisdom: Remember, LACES means
> Lookout, Awareness, Communication, Escape, and
> Safety. It's your template for travel safety.**

Threat Assessment

**Threat assessment is identifying dangers or unpleasant
surprises at your destination.** Threat assessments are part of
your planning. Research questions such as:

1. What are the current events? (Are there political demonstrations, citizen unrest, terrorism warnings, etc.?)
2. What are the laws in your destination country? (Possession of alcohol, erotic pictures, or an adult video is a serious crime in some countries.)
3. What is the country's attitude toward Americans?
4. Will a country tolerate your religious practices?
5. What's the country's criminal history? (In some areas of the world, kidnapping is a cottage industry.)

Travel Wisdom: Check with the U.S. Department of State (DOS) for travel warnings at http://travel.state.gov.

When in-country, look for threats and trust your instincts. (This ties back to LACES.) A street or neighborhood that looks bad probably is bad. Beware of unsolicited contacts by people on the street. Check out the transportation system and don't use unofficial cabs or private drivers. Your clothes (especially revealing female attire) or your gestures may cause a threatening situation in some parts of the world.

Fire Safety

Hank has seen many tragedies, as a firefighter, so fire safety is a serious subject. The first step in fire safety is to stay in a sprinklered hotel or cruise ship. A sprinklered ship or hotel (contrary to myth) is safer than the average home.

The awareness, escape, and safe zone elements in **LACES** apply to fire safety. Learn the emergency number in your destination country. If you see or smell smoke in a hotel, call the fire department first. The second call needs to go to the front desk or hotel operator. Many hotels cause delays by sending security personnel to investigate fire calls before calling the fire department. They hate to see BRT's (big red trucks) responding to their front door.

Always Take These Precautions:

Locate at least two exits. This applies to your ship's cabin, hotel, airplane, restaurant, or nightclub. The process is short and simple. Take a few seconds and look for exit signs. Point out the exits to your companions.

Have your clothes ready by your bed including shoes, flashlight, room key, and a jacket. Get dressed and head for the door if the fire alarm sounds. If there's smoke in your room, stay low, don't stand up. Have your exit plan in mind.

> **Personal Experience: Hank often declines a 12th-floor room in a hotel. He asks for something on the 6th floor or below. Fire ladders do not reach above the seventh or eighth floor.**

Feel your door (especially the knob) for heat before exiting. Look for smoke entering around the door. Crack the door and look into the hallway. The lights may be out, so have your flashlight ready. Close your door behind you and head for the stairwell exit. *Never take the elevator.* If there is heavy smoke in the hallway, crawl to the exit. Visibility is better and smoke is less dense at the floor level.

Stay in your room if your escape route is blocked by smoke or heat. Call for help by dialing the appropriate digit for an outside dial tone and then dialing the emergency number (it's not 9-1-1 outside the U.S.). Tell the operator or dispatcher the name of your hotel, and the address. Tell them you are trapped and give your floor and room number. Note: Emergency numbers differ throughout the world. For example, in Japan, the emergency number is 119 for fire/EMS and 110 for police; in the U.K. it's 999; in France it's 15 for EMS, 18 for fire, and 17 for police.

Prevent smoke from entering your room by shutting off the air conditioning system and closing or blocking

air/heat vents. Fill your bathtub with water, wet the towels, and use them to seal the cracks around the door. Try to avoid breaking your windows, especially if you're above the fire. Broken windows allow smoke to enter from the outside. Leaning out of a window to get a breath is a last resort.

> **Travel Wisdom: Don't delay your exit when you hear a fire alarm or smell smoke. Get to an exit door or stairwell—it's critical.**

People often ask about advertised escape masks. There was no escape mask on the market approved by the National Institute of Safety and Health as of 2003. Beware of advertising claims that use the word "tested." Tested does not mean certified or approved. Currently, escape masks and hoods (including military surplus masks) offer temporary protection at best. None of these devices work in a low-oxygen atmosphere.

Health and Medical

Maintaining fitness and a healthy lifestyle at home is the first step to travel health. If you're overweight and/or a smoker, you tire easily and are more susceptible to disease or injury. This isn't a fitness book, so we'll quit lecturing . . . enough said.

Include a health plan in your travel plan. Consult your physician if you have medical conditions affected by travel. Remember to make a list of required medications, and fill your prescriptions before you hit the road.

> **Travel Wisdom: Carry controlled drugs in their prescription bottles. You can be arrested for illegal drugs in some countries if you carry certain drugs that are not in their prescription container. If in doubt, take a copy of your prescription.**

Other Medical Considerations;
- **If you have a serious medical condition, carry a medical card written in the language of your destination country.** Foreign paramedics and medical personnel may not be able to read your medical bracelet or necklace.

  Foreign travel may require specific immunizations. Research immunization requirements months in advance. Some immunizations require a series of shots given weeks apart. **An excellent information source is the Centers for Disease Control (CDC). The CDC website address is www.cdc.gov. It provides excellent and reliable information about worldwide disease threats and immunization requirements.**

- **Bring over-the-counter medications for common medical problems.** Pack small amounts of these items in your carry-on bag. Wash your hands frequently, especially after using the restroom and before/after eating. Use anti-bacterial hand gel frequently. Many illnesses and infections are transmitted from your hands to your mouth, nose or eyes. Consult your physician about taking antibiotics. The medical field is concerned about arbitrary antibiotic use, especially when the antibiotics are taken as a preventive medication.

- **Find out about the medical facilities in your destination countries.** Many developing nations may not have the medical facilities you take for granted in the United States or Europe. In most developing countries, the water is not safe to drink. Untreated water causes diarrhea (sometimes called Montezuma's Revenge), and dysentery in severe cases. A result is dehydration, abdominal cramps and possibly death in extreme exposures. At the least, you'll be an unhappy camper.

  The best way to avoid the discomfort and complications from unsafe water is to drink only bottled water from a safe source. Be careful about ordering salads (they may be

washed with contaminated water). Brush your teeth with
bottled water.

On the Street

The street is any place that's outside. Avoid walking alone
on the street if possible. If you are a single traveler, hook up
with a small group. In a group, there are more lookouts and
safety in numbers. On the other hand, crowds of Americans
and Europeans (inside or on the street) are possible terrorism
targets. Our advice: Stay in a small group. Odds are that street
crime, not terrorism, is your biggest threat.

Mugging and theft are the most common street crimes.
Street professionals can unzip a purse or fanny pack, or lift a
wallet without you noticing. They're adept at cutting a purse
strap or cutting the bottom of a fanny pack or backpack and
taking your goodies. These people have plenty of time to
practice. Stealing from you is their lucrative full-time job.

Street Smarts

**A small travel pouch for cash and credit cards is safer
than a wallet or purse.** Wear the pouch on a neck strap and
tuck it into your shirt or blouse. A money belt is another
effective device. Money is stored in a zippered compartment
inside the belt. Beware of carrying valuables in a backpack;
you cannot see the pack . . . or what's going on behind you.

If you carry a wallet, put it in your front pocket. This
method isn't totally effective . . . a good pickpocket can still
get it. Place a rubber band around your wallet or place a small
comb sideways into it. This makes it harder for someone to
slide it out of your pocket.

**Carry a "throw-away" wallet in a back pocket with
several one-dollar bills and some fake credit cards.** Use
cards without a name or address on them; they look official
and make the wallet thicker. If you get mugged, throw this

wallet on the ground and run in the opposite direction. (You remembered LACES, so you have a safe zone in mind).

Guard your luggage, especially in crowded terminals. Keep your hands on your suitcase or put your foot through the strap. Having your suitcase near you is not enough. When you are distracted by a conversation or cell phone call, your suitcase "walks" away. When seated, put your bags in front of you, not beside you. You can tie a bell to your bag. (Personally, I'd go crazy if I had to hear a bell ring every time I moved my bag.).

Beware of local people on the street or drivers who offer to help you. Don't get into a car with an unsolicited guide. Book personal guides through the Internet or your travel agent. Check references. Learn the difference between official cabs and "gypsy" cabs. If you are suspicious of your driver get out near a crowded location or hotel, pay the driver, and get another cab. Be especially cautious of cabs in Mexico and South America.

In the Air

Air security begins when you enter the airport. Watch your bags and take the precautions discussed in the section on theft. Your bags are most vulnerable when going through security screening. Do not place your bags on the x-ray conveyor belt until the person in front of you has cleared the metal detector. A trick for baggage thieves is to stall and create a delay in front of you. Meanwhile an accomplice on the other side removes your bags that passed through.

You greatly enhance your chances of quickly clearing security by placing metal objects, pagers, keys, change, and cell phones in your carry bag. Avoid wearing jewelry and large metal belt buckles. Do not pack wrapped gifts, and don't travel with prohibited objects. Obviously, you know not to pack knives or guns. However, did you know that you can't take a baseball bat, pool cue, or hockey stick on an aircraft? Consult the Transportation Security Administration website at **www.tsa.gov**. TSA also has an informative program called Prepare for Takeoff on the Internet at **www.TSATravelTips.us**.

Keeping your seatbelt fastened during taxiing and in flight is the one most important flight safety step. Remember that unexpected turbulence happens on a clear day. Another important safety step is knowing your exits. Look around and note at least two separate exits. Read the passenger information card in the seatback in front of you for exit instructions and diagrams. Learn how to open exit doors and windows. Count the rows between your seat and the exit. Visibility will be poor in an emergency. (**LACES** again).

Situational awareness during take-off and landing is important. Look out the window to keep track of the aircraft's attitude; this isn't the time for reading or sleeping. Keep your shoes on and have a pocket flashlight. Be ready to move fast if there's a landing or take-off accident.

During an in-flight emergency, listen to the flight crew. If Sky Marshals are involved in an incident (unlikely), follow their instructions immediately.

Buses, Cars, and Trains

Study the transit system at your destination before you travel. Determine what modes of transportation are available. Familiarization with the system routes and schedules will make your trip less confusing.

Buses and trains have emergency exits different from aircraft. These exits include removable windows and additional exit doors. Train exits vary widely throughout the world. For example, the middle doors on the train cars in the D.C. Metro System are emergency doors, but this doesn't apply everywhere. Avoid the lead or trailing car on commuter trains. They are more likely to be severely damaged in a collision accident. Remember that your flashlight may save your life in a dark tunnel or nighttime accident.

Finally . . . The Hotel!

Many of the fire safety steps and the **LACES** principle apply to hotels. Start by checking out the lobby. Take a quick look and identify the exits. Look at the people "hanging out" in the lobby. Ask the concierge and the desk clerk about walking in the local area. Ask what neighborhoods or streets should be avoided.

Check out the hallway on the way to your room. If you feel that you're being followed, go back to the lobby and request a security escort to your room. Don't open your room door when there is a suspicious person nearby in the hallway. Don't immediately walk into your room. Take 30 seconds to be safe. Begin by propping the door open with your bag (your LACES escape route) and turning on the lights. Leave a travel companion right outside the door (your LACES lookout). Check the closets and the bathroom as you walk into the room. When everything's clear, return to the door, get your bag, and lock the door.

Do not accept unsolicited room service or unexpected deliveries. Call the front desk if someone claims to have a room service surprise. Instruct delivery people (through your locked door) to leave packages or gifts at the front desk. If anyone appears suspicious, call security.

Don't leave valuables unsecured in your room. Use the room safe or the front desk safe. Lastly, carry a card with the hotel address, especially in foreign-language countries. You can hand the card to a cab driver to get you back to the hotel. Also carry a card from the hotel in your pocket when you are not with your companions. If you are involved in an accident, the card will alert authorities where to notify fellow travelers.

A cruise ship is a floating hotel. A sprinklered ship (like a hotel) is very safe. Hotel safety principles apply to ships. Fire is the single biggest threat on a cruise ship. It's important to learn the exits from your cabin and below deck areas. Don't forget to set up a muster site like we discussed earlier. Remember the location of your muster station and lifeboat station. Take the mandatory lifeboat drill on your cruise seriously. Learn how to wear your cabin life vest, and note additional deck storage areas for life vests. A lifeboat evacuation is extremely rare, but of course, extremely serious. Be prepared for that rare day. Dress for the weather (especially if it's cold), and bring your medications and a flashlight. Snacks and bottled water is also a good idea. Always follow crew instructions.

Sometimes ships encounter heavy seas. Keep track of approaching weather and take your seasick medication ahead of time. Stay off outside decks that are wet, pitching, and rolling. Remember that high winds make outside doors difficult to open and cause doors to slam. This is not the time for alcohol consumption. If you are walking impaired, restrict your movement to avoid falling.

> **Personal Experience: In the fall of 2002 we cruised Prins Christian Sund, Greenland, in smooth seas. Hours later, we had to change course to outrun Hurricane Gustav. We had 25-foot seas for two days. For us it was an adventure; for some it was an ordeal.**

Terrorism

No place in the world is immune from terrorism. However, your odds of being a terrorism victim are extremely low. Those odds are further reduced if you take some precautions. LACES definitely applies to terrorism, especially the lookout and awareness principles. The more you are aware of potential dangers, the less likely you will have to plan and escape to a safe zone.

Researching your destination is important. Avoid travel to countries on the State Department travel warning list. This list changes frequently. In 1999 we had a great trip to the paradise of Bali. After the 2002 nightclub bombing, Bali was declared a travel hazard. Our trip also included exotic Lombok. A month later, Christians were fleeing that island's Islamic extremists. Changes in government, revolutions, and political coups take place throughout the world. Stable areas become unstable quickly. Do your homework before your trip. Stay informed!

Words of Encouragement

Please don't let this chapter scare you! Yes, twenty-first century life has risks. However, the odds of a long life are in your favor. By taking precautions, you increase those odds. Safety is low cost and requires only a few hours of planning, and a few minutes during each travel day. Stay alert. Stay safe . . . and get out there and have fun!

CHAPTER SIX

MINDING YOUR TRAVEL MANNERS

You can get through life with bad manners, but it's easier with good manners.

- Lillian Gish

This chapter is near and dear to our hearts. No one likes to be stereotyped as a "Tacky Tourist" . . . or worse, an "Ugly American." Yet, we often see travelers who are probably polite, pleasant and patient at home behave and dress in ways that are inappropriate and offensive to fellow travelers and especially to people of other cultures.

For example, on a recent trip to Hong Kong, an older woman on one of our tours was complaining loudly at breakfast about how tired she was of the "funny money, funny food, and funny accents" of the Chinese. Surrounded by Chinese diners and restaurant workers, her comments were inconsiderate and rude. Sadly, she did not realize how her comments were perceived—and that our American food, dollars and accents are equally "funny" to foreign guests in the United States.

Many travelers don't take the time to understand and appreciate the customs and cultural differences of their travel destination. Unfortunately others seem to feel they don't have to adjust their behavior . . . after all, they are paying good money for service. You can bet these same folks are offended by travelers acting inappropriately on their turf. We live in a wonderfully diverse world. One of the greatest benefits of travel is the opportunity to experience different customs and lifestyles.

If we are unable or unwilling to take the time to study, accommodate and appreciate diversity, why travel?

Basic Do's and Don'ts of Travel Etiquette.

- **Take the time to learn about your destination.** It's easy and interesting to research different lifestyles, cultural sensitivities, and customs. The Internet puts the world at your fingertips. If you are not a web surfer, there are guidebooks on virtually every destination that include appreciating the diversity of your destination. Please understand and embrace the concept that just because something is different it is not wrong.

> **Travel Wisdom: Check out *The Simple Guide to Customs & Etiquette* books. These handy little guides introduce you to the unique customs and etiquette of worldwide travel destinations.**

- **Although English is spoken in most parts of the world (much better than we speak other languages), don't expect to be understood in every case.** When communication is difficult, slow down. It's not necessary to speak loudly. The person may not understand the words you are saying, but they are not hard of hearing. Don't refer to their accents or language as funny, weird or odd. As part of your travel research, learn to speak a few words in the native language of your destination—especially the correct words for "please" and "thank you." Even if your pronunciation isn't perfect, your effort will be appreciated.

- **Think before you speak.** You may be tempted to criticize or make jokes about something, believing the listeners don't speak English. Humor is frequently misunderstood or misinterpreted. You never know who knows even a few words . . . the ones you don't want understood. It's best to refrain from making jokes or disparaging remarks about other people or other customs. As Grandmother said, "If you can't say something nice, don't say anything!"

- **Dress appropriately.** We watched many "tacky tourists" being turned away at The Vatican because they were dressed in shorts and tank tops. Your dress sends a strong message. Leave your Bevis and Butthead T-shirt at home. Unless you are in a resort area or on a cruise ship, shorts will also mark you as a tourist and restrict admission to many shrines, temples, and cathedrals as well as many restaurants and theatre performances. When in doubt, err on the side of a conservative appearance.

- **Practice good photo etiquette.** Travelers often snap rolls and rolls of film, from speeding tour buses, at performances, of men, women and children on the street. Although flash photography and video are almost always restricted at performances and museums, inevitably someone can't resist snapping a photo. Constant flashes are distracting to performers and irritating to others in the audience. The photographs rarely develop properly since the avid photographer's flash is at too great a distance from the subject.

Snapping photos or video of private corporate locations may violate the law. Taking photos or video of government or high-security areas is asking for trouble. Snapping photos or video of people without their consent violates personal privacy—and in some cultures may create an international incident! Ask before you aim the camera or video. Don't be surprised if the enterprising subject of your photo requests payment for their service as your model. Pay graciously or put the camera on hold!

- **Hold the cigar, the chewing gum, and the noisy beepers/ cell phones.** Good etiquette abroad and at home. Although cigar smoking seems to be the latest cool craze, the odor and smoke are offensive to many others breathing the same air. While it may seem the perfect ending for a good meal, lighting up a cigar, even in outdoor spaces, can spoil another person's meal. Be a considerate smoker. Seek out a smoking location that doesn't impact non-smokers.

     Park the chewing gum. Not only is smacking and popping plain bad manners, in some countries (Singapore being one) chewing gum is illegal. In fact, in Singapore littering of any type, candy papers, cigarette butts, etc., is strictly forbidden. Violators, including tourists, incur heavy fines.

- **Actions do speak louder than words.** Gestures and other forms of non-verbal communications differ greatly from culture to culture. Ironically, a positive gesture used commonly in America may be offensive in another country. Former President George Bush, Sr. learned this the hard way. Boarding Air Force One in Australia, he turned to the crowd, smiling broadly and gave them a good ole' American "thumbs up." In Australia, the thumbs up gesture is the equivalent of giving someone "the finger" in the U.S. The Australians were not impressed or amused by his faux pas.

     Another commonly used American gesture, making a circle with the thumb and index finger (the OK sign), has negative connotations in many other cultures. In France, it symbolizes that something is worthless. In Spain, Greece and the CIS (Russian Federation) it is viewed as "giving someone the finger." In Latin America, it refers to a bodily orifice. In Japan, the OK sign is a symbol of money, a way of requesting coins as change.

Examples of Gestures with Different Cultural Interpretations
- **In Africa and many other countries, crossing the legs, especially when the soles of the feet show, is considered an insult.**
- **Pointing or beckoning with the index finger is a gesture used only with animals in Asia and many other countries.**
- **Folded arms are viewed as a sign of arrogance in parts of Europe.**
- **Eating everything on your plate (Clean Plate Club) implies your host did not provide enough food in Latin America, Africa, and parts of Asia.**
- **In the Middle East and Latin America if you comment on and admire another person's possession, they may feel obligated to give it to you and be offended if you refuse it.**
- **Nodding your head may mean "no" instead of "yes," in Malaysia and India.**

Confused yet? Gestures, greetings, eye contact, personal space and table manners are all forms of communication that enhance or detract from personal perceptions. While they may seem confusing and confounding, taking the time and effort to learn the most basic travel manners for your destination shows respect and prevents misunderstanding and misconceptions.

The age-old **Golden Rule** says **"Do unto others as you would have them do unto you."** The trouble with the Golden Rule is that it assumes others want to be treated as you do. When it comes to travel, or any interpersonal relationship, the **"Platinum Rule"** says **"Do unto others as they would have you do unto them."** Give it some thought. Treating others appropriately by their standards can have dramatic effects.

(See our Resource Chapter for resources on travel etiquette.)

If you wish to travel far and fast, travel light, take off your envies,   jealousies, unforgiveness, and fears.
-Glenn Clark

CHAPTER SEVEN

TAKING CARE OF BUSINESS

Unlike eagerly anticipated vacation travel, business travel is a corporate fact of life. A frequent business traveler rarely describes a trip as "fun." On the contrary, most business travelers view business travel as a punishment, not a perk . . . with dread, not delight.

Hank travels on business at a "platinum level." His business travel attitude ranges from disgusted to tolerant to (on occasion) enjoyable. Between my years as a flight attendant and Hank's business travel experience we've discovered some tested and true ways to make business travel easier—and less stressful.

Business Air Travel

When it comes to air travel, the best advice is to lower your expectations. Don't expect to depart or arrive on time. Don't expect your checked bag to arrive when you do. And, certainly don't expect much, if anything, in the way of food and beverages.

Smart business travelers use pre-planning to reduce business travel woes:

- **Join frequent flyer programs** for all airlines you travel with . . . even those you use on an "infrequent" basis. There is some amount of clout associated with frequent flyer membership. Use websites such as **www.webflyer.com** to track current promotions for bonus miles and other benefits.
- **If your travel budget permits, join airline airport clubs.** They are a "safe haven" amidst the chaos of crowded gate areas. Other advantages of club membership include: a safe place to store your carry-on bag while you walk around the airport, special check-in and flight assistance, Internet access, meeting rooms, and often complimentary cocktails and snacks.
- **Book as early as possible.** Obviously, this isn't possible with last-minute business travel, but early booking always offers more arrival and departure options and better seating. For last-minute trips, when a fare is quoted, always ask about Internet specials that might be available. Airline reservations agents never "offer" you an Internet special fare, but will often give you one if you ask for it.
- **Book departures as early in the day as possible.** "The later in the day, the longer the delay" seems to be an airline rule.
- **Avoid booking the last flight of the day.** If it cancels or you miss it, you are stuck!
- **Become an expert in airline websites.** Look at all scheduling options in addition to the flight you're booking. Use seat maps to select your seat. (Choose an aisle seat, preferably in the exit row, for more legroom and convenience of getting up during the flight.) Check delays and cancellations. Print airport maps so you know the lay of the land when you are changing airlines or terminals in unfamiliar airports.
- **Even if you're a Palm Pilot fan, print your itinerary and listings of flight options in case your flight is delayed or**

cancelled and your Palm Pilot fails. Assume something will go wrong with your schedule and always have Plan B.

- **Pre-program airline reservation numbers in your cell phone.** When a delay or cancellation occurs, don't run with the crowd to stand in a long ticket counter line and get re-booked. Quickly, call Reservations directly to re-book. Seats are limited. Time is critical when there is a delay.

- **If you're a "preferred class traveler" you will get the opportunity to board first** and have room for your carry-on in the overhead bins. If not an early boarder, avoid seating at the front of coach cabin. By the time you board, all the overhead space will be filled. Request seating over the wing. There are several advantages to the over-wing area. On most airplanes, these seats are in an emergency row. Also, you'll still have overhead space available when you board. Avoid seating in the rear of the airplane. In the event of delayed arrival and a short connection, you're stuck in the back waiting impatiently while passengers slowly retrieve their belongings to get off.

- **Avoid checking a bag!** Plan ahead. Pack smart. Carry on your luggage. You'll avoid the frustration of fighting the crowd in baggage claim. You'll be sure you have your bag . . . that it's not in Tulsa while you are in Tucson.

- **Ship purchases or presentations** ahead of time to avoid juggling them with your carry-on and clearing security with extra, possibly prohibited, items.

- **Keep travel-sized cosmetic/personal-hygiene products in a travel utility bag,** including over-the-counter medications and prescriptions. Make this your business travel bag and leave it in your carry-on between trips. Re-stock immediately after each trip and never be caught short with mid-night heartburn and no remedy.

- **Bring your own in-flight culinary delights.** Airline food is practically non-existent except on long flights. Even then, it leaves much to be desired. Traveling for business or pleasure, we always bring refreshments such as: snack bars, apples or pears, cheese and crackers, and frequently a gourmet deli-sandwich or salad. We were almost attacked by hungry passengers on a delayed flight when we brought out our barbecue sandwiches. It also pays to keep a bottle of water tucked in your carry-on or briefcase.

- **On long flights stash an inflatable neck pillow and foam earplugs in your carry-on.** Airline seats are uncomfortable. A few personal amenities ease the discomfort of a long night in the sky.
- **Get to know and be courteous to your local ticket agents.** They can occasionally bend rules and help resolve travel problems. Bring them treats occasionally. Subtle bribery works.
- **Make the most of flight time.** Keep a note pad or mini-voice recorder with you to catch ideas that pop up. Take along good reading material. Go for lightweight paperbacks and magazines that can be left behind when finished. Take a much-needed nap . . . especially if you have a chatty seatmate.
- **Know your rights.** Study **Rule 240.** When you encounter a flight delay, ask the reason. If the reason cited is weather or traffic delays (known as force majeure events), check with other airlines and see if they are having the same delays. If the delay is **not** weather or air traffic related, ask to be re-booked on the next flight or even a competing airline. Often all you have to say to the agent is "Can you 240 me?" and he/she will know you know your rights. Rule 240 also applies to getting "bumped" on over-sold flights. Get a copy and keep it with you. See ***Travel Resources*** for websites with copies of Rule 240 for most major airlines.

Logistics of Ground Transportation

Plan your ground transportation ahead of time. Most major cities have private shuttle/limo service from airports to hotels.

Rather than taking an airport shuttle bus that makes numerous stops or taking your chances on the quality and safety of taxi transport, book a car and driver and have them waiting on arrival. Book the same service for returning to the airport from the hotel. For example, we've found that a Lincoln Town Car from Newark into Manhattan costs only slightly more than a taxi and is a much more enjoyable ride.

Even though you may have to rent a car for business in some cities, car rental is a guaranteed stress factor in business travel. You can count on waiting for the car rental shuttle, waiting in lines, reservation mix-ups, getting lost in strange cities, parking problems, and the aggravation of adding time to your departure in turning the car back in.

The best way to avoid all this added stress is to avoid renting a car unless it is absolutely necessary. Most major cities offer a wide variety of local transportation options at a fraction of the cost of car rental. Many conference centers and resorts cater to non-driving business travelers with free shuttles, not only to and from the airport, but to local restaurants and shopping centers.

Travel Wisdom: If your office utilizes a corporate travel planner, he or she should maintain a current file of business travel locations. This file should include: recommended hotels, modes of ground transportation, convenient restaurants, and other relevant information to assist you during your trip.

If you have to have your own wheels, try these tips to smooth the way:

- **As with frequent flyers, membership has benefits.** Car club members by-pass check-in and checkout lines, gain frequent flyer mileage and upgrade points.
- **Book early and keep good records.** Get confirmation in writing. Re-confirm your reservation. Be aware you can

come up short (car-less) if there is an airline delay and available cars are not turned in, and turned over, on time. Back to having a Plan B.

- **Know your insurance benefits**. Do you need the rental car collision? You need coverage, but avoid duplicating expenses.
- **Print maps** from the Internet in advance and don't leave the parking lot before you have a clear idea of where you're going and the best route for getting there.

The Roof Over Your Business Head

Choosing the best business hotel means knowing what you want and expect in a business hotel. Location, price, and amenities are factors in choosing the business hotel that meets your travel needs.

Make sure your corporate travel planner (assistant or office manager) or travel agent knows exactly what criteria are important to you in selecting the right lodging. For instance, if you travel with a laptop, you won't need to pay for business center services such as fax and email. You will need an Internet connection in your room. If you never eat breakfast, the complimentary buffet breakfast is an amenity priced into your room that you can do without. On an extended trip, a hotel room grows smaller by the day, a suite or mini-suite adds to your comfort and reduces stress. Our favorite hotels on extended business trips are Embassy Suites, Hampton Suites, or other chain "suites."

If you are responsible for your own travel arrangements, stick to national hotel chains you recognize until you learn the lay of the land. Research hotels on the Internet and get a good idea of location, room layout, transportation needs, and amenities. Most major hotel chains also offer web-only deals. Register online as a frequent guest and include your preferences such as non-smoking, king or double beds, and credit card information. Frequent guest amenities such as free nights and merchandise add up like frequent flyer miles. Take advantage of the benefits you accrue while on the road and in the air.

Mixing Business With Pleasure

Yes, business travel is tedious—stressful. But, with a little creative thought and planning, you can add an element of pleasure to virtually any business trip.

Hank travels on business at least thirty times per year. He has learned that in between flights and business appointments, there are opportunities to add pleasure to his business trips.

First, whenever possible, I accompany him on business trips. Yes, I am fortunate to be in a position where I have the flexibility to "tag along." And, our children are grown, there is no longer a childcare consideration. Sometimes we use frequent flyer mileage for my ticket. Other times, when ticket prices are competitive, we opt to pay the fare.

When I tag along, I plan daytime activities, such as cooking classes, for me. We plan special evening meals or even "in house" picnics for some evenings.

When I don't accompany Hank, he has these tips for making a trip less tedious:

Catch up with old friends and acquaintances in the area. Many of his best business contacts have come from spur-of-the-moment contacts with long-lost friends and associates.

Seek out unique entertainment. You have two choices after business hours. Sit in your room or go to the bar. Opt out on both and utilize websites and other resources to find entertainment to add a fun element to your business travel. Hank often discovers a theatre production or sports event in the city he is traveling to.

Exercise is important while traveling. If you are a walker or runner, check with the front desk as to the safety of the area and get out there and enjoy the fresh air. If your hotel has a gym or you have membership in a national chain, take advantage of travel time to get in a few fitness hours.

Adding a little pleasure to business reduces the stress and strain of business travel.

CHAPTER EIGHT

THE DISABLED TRAVELER

Accessible travel for people with disabilities has improved significantly in recent years. Legislation, such as the Americans with Disabilities Act and the Air Carriers Access Act, has encouraged the travel industry to update inadequate facilities and train personnel to assist travelers with special needs.

That said, accessible accommodations cannot be assumed. As always, planning and advance preparation are the keys to a positive travel experience. Objectively examine limitations inherent to individual disability. There are many types of disabilities. Each person's needs are different. Make sure all aspects of travel from airline seats to tour buses to hotel rooms and cruise ships are capable of meeting your unique needs. Know your rights as a disabled traveler. But, be prepared to encounter some snags along the way.

Airline Accessibility

Legislation establishes air travel guidelines to ensure persons with disabilities can travel without discrimination. These guidelines include:

- A carrier may not refuse transportation to a passenger solely on the basis of a disability.
- Carriers may not limit the number of people with disabilities on a flight.
- Carriers must accommodate passengers with disabilities even if that person is an inconvenience to crewmembers and other passengers.

However, there are important exceptions and special rules that apply to travelers with certain diseases and disabilities:
- The individual with the disability cannot endanger the health or safety of other passengers.
- Legislation does not apply to International carriers.
- If the aircraft has less than thirty seats, the carrier may refuse transportation that involves lifts and other boarding devices that cannot be accommodated by small aircraft.

If you are booking your own flight through airline reservations or via the Internet, don't assume (always a dangerous thing with travel) the flight you book can accommodate your needs. Look at seating logistics, aircraft storage facilities, lavatory accessibility, special equipment needs, and availability of boarding and deplaning assistance.

Airlines may require up to **48 hours** notice for passengers requiring any of the following:
- Wheelchair provision and assistance.
- Provisions for carrying any hazardous materials.
- Accommodations for a group of ten or more disabled passengers.

Be aware that airlines are not required to provide any of the following:
- Medical oxygen on board. (Except for emergency use.)
- Carriage of an incubator.

- Hook up for a respirator.
- Accommodations for a passenger requiring a stretcher.

Airlines also may require a travel companion or aide when a passenger is unable to comprehend or respond to safety instructions and procedures or is unable to assist with his or her own evacuation from the aircraft. Although airline personnel are trained to assist disabled travelers with boarding and deplaning, opening food packages, assistance to and from lavatories (but not inside the lavatory), and with loading and storing onboard equipment, travelers often have to wait for assistance and find personnel training inadequate. You know your capabilities and challenges. Despite legislation and policies, be realistic with travel expectations.

Hotel Accessibility

Again, legislation applies, but don't assume anything. When booking hotel accommodations, always call the hotel directly . . . not the 1-800 central reservations number. The person you talk to at 1-800 is probably not in the same city as the hotel, has never even seen the rooms, and may rely on outdated or inaccurate information about accessibility. Ask the person you call for very specific information about room and property accessibility. If they can't provide accurate information, ask to speak to someone in housekeeping or maintenance who works inside the room on a regular basis. If you stop at a hotel without an advance reservation, ask to see the room before you check-in. No surprises that way!

> **Travel Wisdom: When you reserve a room with your credit card be certain that it is specifically an accessible room . . . not just any room. Ask for written confirmation. Double check a few days before arrival.**

As with air travel, know your rights. If you find the accessible room you reserved is not available, the hotel is required to find an accessible room for you...even at another hotel. You can bet they will not volunteer this service. It's up to you to know and exercise your rights.

Cruise Line Accessibility

Of all types of travel, cruises are one of the best ways for a disabled traveler and their companion to enjoy travel with minimal hassle and maximum benefits. But, as always, do your research. Newer and larger ships are much more accessible than older, smaller ships. Older ships usually have narrow doors, doorsills that block wheelchairs, or elevated bathroom facilities that are not accessible.

Some of the areas you need to question include:
- Accessible embarkation and debarkation at all ports.
- Accessibility of public areas of the ships, such as theaters and lounges.
- Cabin door widths and flat (no sill) entrances.
- Bathroom accessibility/accommodations, (i.e., roll-in showers and raised toilet seats.)
- Electrical outlets for re-charging wheelchair batteries.
- Assistance available for shore excursions.
- Medical releases required for travel.
- Medical oxygen availability and restrictions.
- Handling of service animals.
- Medical facilities and level of care available onboard.

Ports of call also require research. Ports that require the use of a small boat (tender) to go ashore may not be able to accommodate wheelchairs . . . especially in rough seas. Small ports may not have lifts to assist disabled passengers in boarding and disembarking. Sidewalks and streets may be cobblestones and impassable in a wheelchair or tour buses may not be accessible. Remember, once you are in international territory, U.S. legislation does not apply.

Travel Wisdom: Find a travel agent who specializes in working with disabled travelers. They know what cruise lines, ships and ports can accommodate your needs and offer an enjoyable experience for you and your travel companion.

Fifty million Americans are living with disabilities; statistics show that approximately 75% of them travel . . . some frequently and afar. The more you travel, the easier it gets. The travel bug bites everyone. With advance planning, preparation and practice you'll be ready to take advantage of travel opportunities when wanderlust strikes.

(See additional resources for disabled travelers in our Favorite Resource Chapter.)

CHAPTER NINE

GOING SOLO

The rewards of the journey far outweigh the risk of leaving the harbor.

- Unknown

I am amazed at how many people express a desire to travel . . . followed by "But I don't have anyone to go with." A person may not have a ready travel companion for many reasons, most commonly death, divorce or disinterest. Whatever the reason, you have three choices.

One: stay home and read about travel.
Two: try to find a travel companion.
Three: take the plunge and go alone!

And yes, it is more enjoyable to have a significant other with whom to share a beautiful sunset and marvel over spectacular sights. That said, don't miss out on wonderful opportunities to see the world simply because there is no one at your side every minute.

When I first began traveling with the airlines, it was a big challenge for me to go out alone. We would arrive in New York City or Boston for an overnight layover. Other crewmembers had friends or relatives to visit or would choose to sleep the layover away. I quickly learned that if I truly wanted to see the world, I'd better get used to getting out alone sometimes. I was pleasantly surprised at how easy it was to meet people when I traveled alone. It didn't take long to feel confident and comfortable eating alone in a fine restaurant or enjoying a glass of champagne at a sidewalk café. I would have missed so much if I had allowed lack of companions to hold me back.

FIVE GOOD THINGS ABOUT TRAVELING SOLO

1. You enjoy the freedom of doing exactly what you want . . . when you want.
2. You meet new friends easily. People hesitate to approach couples or groups.
3. You gain self-confidence and an appreciation for your own resources.
4. You can change your plans at a moment's notice without anyone's approval.
5. You don't have to listen to anyone snivel, sneer or snore.

We meet many men and women traveling alone. Invariably, they express enjoyment in their single travel and share some great independent travel wisdom.

Top Ten Tips for Solo Travel

1. **Do your homework.** Buy guidebooks written specifically for solo travelers. (Check out *Travel Alone & Love It: A Flight Attendant's Guide to Solo Travel* by Sharon Wingler.) Research Internet sites for solo travelers. Take a look at **www.journeywoman.com and www.gutsywomentravel.com.** Read reviews and stories from other solo travelers.

2. **Start small.** If you have no experience going alone or you've never dined out at a table for one, begin with a dinner out at a fine restaurant in your hometown. If you feel self-conscious, bring along some reading material or a journal. Order a glass of wine, enjoy people watching, and reading a book with an intriguing title. Don't be surprised if someone strikes up a conversation. Once you feel comfortable dining alone, try a day trip or an overnight stay. Learn when and where you feel comfortable and your confidence will grow with each new venture.

3. **Travel alone with a group.** Booking travel with a tour group allows you to travel solo, but still be with other people. You can have your privacy and independence and enjoy the security and social aspects of being a member of the group for city tours and evening functions. You can opt out if the group activities don't appeal to you and you want a quiet day or evening alone.

   Specialty travel is one of the fastest-growing areas of the travel industry and is perfect for solo travelers. Specialty travel tailors trips for travelers with specific interests. Ranging from art to zoology, there is a specialty tour for you. Even though you are traveling alone, since travel is focused on related tours and activities, you automatically have something in common with fellow travelers. To get an idea of the abundance of special travel tours, check out **www.spectrav.com**. This website contains more than three hundred offerings. Just click on an interest and be amazed at the options available. You may discover an interest you never knew you had! Another equally good specialty travel website is **www.shawguides.com**. Click on an interest and get ready. Cooking classes alone have over five hundred options!

   If you are fifty-five or older, Elderhostel programs also offer wonderful independent travel opportunities. Last year over two hundred fifty thousand travelers took advantage of the unique travel and educational options offered by Elderhostel. Whether you want to stay close to home or venture around the world, you'll find programs and tours for virtually any interest, budget and lifestyle. As with other specialty travel tours, you can travel "alone" in the company of travelers of similar age and interests.

4. **Budget accordingly.** Traveling alone will usually cost more than sharing travel costs with another person. Single supplements apply on cruise lines and with most tour groups. Some agencies advertise "matching you up with a roommate." If your travel budget is limited, this might be an option to consider. We recommend spending more for the single supplement and not taking the risk of an incompatible roomie!

5. **Forget what your mother said about talking to strangers.** Be on the lookout for other single travelers and make the first move. Introduce yourself and invite them to join you for a meal, a couple of coffee or a glass of wine. (Talking to strangers does *not* include "real" strangers on the street. Talk to strangers only in safe locations. Personal safety should always be foremost in your mind.)

On a recent transatlantic cruise, we met several interesting single cruisers who joined us at our table for the breakfast buffet or evening shows. Cruises are a great way to travel alone, see the world, and make new acquaintances in a safe environment. Last year, we persuaded a close friend to cruise Alaska alone. Her spouse didn't want to travel and she badly needed to get away and relax. She enjoyed the experience so much, she booked another cruise this year . . . this time to Europe.

Years ago, my flight attendant roommate and I met another woman traveling alone in the airport in Spain. After striking up a conversation, she altered her itinerary and joined us for the next two weeks. We kept in touch for many years afterward. Main point: When you travel alone, it's up to you to overcome shyness and reach out to others. You will be rewarded with many new friends and memorable travel experiences.

6. **Educate yourself on your dream destination.** Every culture has a protocol for single travelers . . . especially women traveling alone. You may not agree with local customs and restrictions, but it is wise to know your destination. Study the local laws, customs, dress, and language. The more you know, the easier it is to enjoy your trip without unnecessary hassles. The more you know, the easier it is to meet others and share your expertise and experience. The more you know, the more you will learn. (Sounds like an oxymoron, but it's true!)

7. **Make sure you can handle your luggage by yourself.** Go for wheeled luggage as checked baggage and a smaller version of a wheeled carry-on bag. Pack as lightly as possible. Don't overload your bag to the point you can't snag it off a baggage carousel. Porters are not always around. There are times you have to "do it yourself!" A carry-on bag should be small enough to fit easily on top of your larger checked bag so you can roll the two as one. As you make purchases along the way, ship them home and keep your load manageable.

8. **Create plans to cope with changes and challenges along the way.** Make certain you have adequate health insurance. Plan your finances to include credit cards, travelers checks and cash (ATM card). Look into ways to keep in touch with family and friends via Internet access or telephone calling cards. When a problem arises, a Plan B reduces stress and increases confidence.

9. **Be ready to feel lonely at times.** There is a big difference between being alone and loneliness. Don't give in to the blues and coop yourself up in a hotel room or cruise cabin, thinking, "Oh poor me." Take a walk. Look for the beauty

around you. Recognize the distinction and make your time alone positive and productive.

10. Be good to yourself. You deserve special luxuries and treats along the way. Treat yourself to a massage . . . a shopping spree . . . a glass of good wine . . . a bubble bath . . . tickets to a hard-to-get theatre show . . . a gourmet cooking class or lecture. Get the idea?

Traveling alone takes practice. The more you travel, the easier it will become. The more you travel alone, the more experiences and opportunities you will discover. Don't sit at home and long for adventure . . . seek it out and savor the moments.

The world is a book, and those who do not travel read only a page.

-Augustine.

CHAPTER TEN

BABY MAKES THREE, OR FOUR, OR MORE

There are only two lasting bequests we can hope to give our children. One of these is roots, the other, wings.
- Hodding Carter

Family travel has such a nice ring to it. A wonderful learning experience. A wonderful bonding opportunity. Memories to last for years. And . . . then there is the commercial that says, "Whoever talked about travel being fun, never traveled with a two-year-old." (Or maybe a teenager.)

We traveled with our sons from the time they were infants on the usual visits to family, to the Grand Canyon and Disneyland, and on several cruises. Our memories run the gamut from the good (even wonderful) to the bad (even ugly). We did some things incredibly right (mostly by accident). We did some things incredibly wrong. We learned a lot. Our sons learned a lot. Looking back, we're glad we have those travel memories—even the not-so-good ones—and wish we had planned and pursued more family travel opportunities. Oh well, there's always grandchildren.

Successful family travel requires experience. We hope you'll benefit from some of our favorite tips and tools for fun and stress-free family travel.

Travel with Twixt Twelve and Twenty

- **Plan ahead.** What's new? Planning applies to all travel. But . . . in this case really, really plan ahead. Involve teen or pre-teen travelers in the planning process. Planning involvement encourages "buy-in" from resistant teens (although resistance is almost obligatory with many teens). Planning offers a disguised learning experience. Planning involvement takes some of the pressure off you.
- **Give specific Internet research assignments**. A close friend gives his two pre-teens the opportunity to uncover travel deals. He invents contests for the best travel deal or the most unusual travel activity with the rewards tied into the trip.
- **If you're traveling with an only child, consider taking along a friend.** Friends are as much an integral part of a teen's life as family (sometimes more). Choose the friend with care and their parental support. Maybe the companion's parents will kick in for their share—after all you are doing them a favor! If not, the minimal added expenses of taking along the "right" teen companion are well worth it!
- **Seek out activities with appeal for everyone**. You will want to enjoy some activities as a group. One good thing about travel with teens . . . you don't **have** to be with them every minute. They certainly won't **want** to be with you every minute. They can go to the Water Park while you attend an art show. Or you can split up and some family members go one way while others go another way.
- **Disguise learning experiences.** One of the best returns we had on travel with our teenaged sons was when our youngest son recently told us (at age twenty-two) how much he *appreciated* (key word that parents love) how he had learned to order and eat properly at high-end restaurants. Many of his friends had no idea how to traverse

the mysteries of silverware in upscale dining. Our sons learned good dining etiquette on cruise ships, reinforced by formal dinners in restaurants and at home.

- **Stay alert.** No matter how much you trust your teen. Check out companions they meet and activities they participate in during travel. When our sons were sixteen and eighteen years old we took them on a seven-day family cruise. While we believe to this day that cruises make a great family vacation, we learned some hard lessons on this cruise.

First mistake: We shared a cabin rather than getting adjoining cabins. Second mistake: We set no curfews. After all what could they possibly get into . . . HA! Third mistake: We were either naïve or too trusting.

Here's the story. There were four hundred high school seniors on the cruise. Our sons thought they had died and gone to heaven. We quickly discovered we had died and gone to hell! There was little, or no, cruise ship supervision. Kids roamed the hallways, drunk and rowdy, all night. They seemed to fall asleep about the time we would normally get up! In Cozumel, we observed kids passed out, being "hauled" back on the ship by their friends.

One night as we passed the casino, we spotted our sixteen-year-old playing blackjack with a drink in hand. When we approached him, he proudly declared he had won over $300.00. It was a week of almost no sleep and lots of parental stress. To top it all off, our sons, proudly sporting long hair and typical teen attire, were hauled aside by Customs for interrogation on arrival home. Thank goodness, no unpleasant consequences ensued. We learned some valuable teen travel lessons from that trip

Be prepared. Know when, where and what your teen is doing. Check out rooms and baggage. Yes . . . snoop! With current travel security and stringent drug laws in foreign countries, don't take any chances. Be safe—not sorry. Protect your teen from himself/herself.

> **TRAVEL NOTE: Since the time of that cruise, cruise lines have tightened security and supervision of young travelers. Most lines do not allow unmarried passengers under twenty-one to travel alone. Almost all the lines have on-board security monitoring legal drinking and gambling ages.**

- **Chill out!** Sounds like the opposite of stay alert, but different meaning. Even the best-laid plans will go awry. Take detours and unexpected changes in stride. Teens will take their lead from you. If you are stressing, they will add to your stress level. If you are flexible and receptive to change and the unexpected, everyone will react accordingly.

Travel with Ages Five to Twelve

This is an optimal age for fun family travel. While school-age kids are relatively independent (can dress and care for themselves), they still have a great sense of curiosity and adventure. They still think you are a brilliant and wonderful parent . . . at least most of the time.

Resorts with active juvenile programs and cruise ships that cater to families are great vacation choices for this age. They have loads of energy and love action. They enjoy being with you and also meeting new travel friends. Your family travel options are abundant.

- **As with teen travelers, offer researching and planning opportunities.** Involve them in selecting activities for family and individual participation.
- **Pack each family member's clothing separately.** If you don't use individual baggage, take advantage of using large Ziplocs (yes, we love Ziplocs!). Pack each day's change

of clothing in a large Ziploc. Makes unpacking and staying organized a breeze.

- **Provide road maps or a world atlas with benchmarks noted**. Helps eliminate the constant "How much farther is it?" and makes a great show 'n tell for school . . . after the trip.
- **Discuss and practice clearing airport security ahead of time to take the uncertainty out of the process and avoid misbehavior.** Check and re-check backpacks and carry-on bags to be sure there are no tools or toys that could be mistaken for weapons. Provide duplicate travel photo identification. You carry one set and have them carry one set.
- **Food and drink are important.** Don't depend on the airlines to provide much in the way of food. Whether flying or traveling by car, relieve frequent requests to stop for treats by bringing them along. Take a treat bag of favorite non-sticky, non-messy snacks and drinks.
- **Provide individual cassette players, portable DVDs, or electronic games to combat roadway or airborne boredom.**
- **Be sure to take medications and medical records for any chronic illnesses**. One of our sons had asthma as a child. We saw the inside of Emergency Rooms almost as often as amusement parks as we traveled.
- **Give everyone a disposable camera.** Expect and enjoy some surprise travel photographs from their unique perspective.
- **Be sure you have a very current photograph of all young travelers, including teens, in case you become separated.** Kids change rapidly at this age. Last year's school photo may not look much like today's kid.
- **Avoid constant pleas for souvenirs by giving each child an allowance of travel mad money** before leaving or the first morning at each destination.

- **Bring along addresses of family and friends and stamps.** Buy loads of postcards for mailing home and travel show 'n tell.
- **Review Chapter Five, Travel Health and Safety, make everyone familiar with LACES.**

Travel with Toddlers and Infants

Once again, really, really plan ahead! There is probably no more difficult age for travel than traveling with a two-year-old. They can't stand being restrained. The notorious "terrible two" temper tantrum surfaces at most inconvenient and embarrassing times. They do not react well to changes in sleeping and eating schedules. Travel is stressful and tiring for you and your young traveler.

- **Try to schedule your travel around nap times.** Hopefully your baby or toddler will fall asleep and awaken as you arrive.
- **Don't count on outside help.** Forget the days when airlines catered to traveling moms and dads. While you may get to board early and may have help carting your vast array of childhood necessities on board, practice juggling baby and bags on your own.
- **Take along at least two changes of clothes for the baby and yourself.** Accidents happen. You may find yourself stuck along the way with a missed or cancelled flight. Pack each day's change of clothes in a Ziploc bag. Take extras for dirty diaper disposal and wet clothing. A large Ziploc can also be a lifesaver as an airsickness bag when nature calls. Make sure you have plenty of diapers and wet wipes, food and formula. Airlines do not provide diapers and you may not find what you need in some airports.
- **Pack small Ziploc bags with favorite snacks for older toddlers.** Pack a few more with surprise toys and treats.

- **Keep a bottle, drink or pacifier handy for take-offs and landings.** Pressure changes bother many babies. Have ears checked prior to travel.
- **Be sure you have documentation for emergencies.** If you are a parent traveling alone, this is not usually a problem. Grandparents and friends traveling with children should be well equipped with a medical power of attorney and medical insurance verification.
- **Check out combination car seat /strollers.** One brand Sit 'N'Stroll retails for around $200.00. It is easy to convert and a lifesaver in more ways than one. For traveling parents, it's must-have. You would never hold your baby in arms unrestrained in an automobile. Holding a baby in an airplane (especially for take-off and landing) is dangerous. If a sudden stop occurs or the flight encounters unexpected severe turbulence, it is almost impossible to keep a firm grip on your baby.
- **Don't forget favorite toys and security blankets.** Guard security blankets with your life. Losing "bunny" or "blankie" results in sleepless nights and major travel trauma!

With planning, patience and a positive outlook, family vacations bring us closer and create memories that last a lifetime. Look for ways to capture and preserve these special memories. Check out *Chapter Eighteen, Making the Memories Last.*

CHAPTER ELEVEN

PROS AND CONS OF GROUP TOURS

The myriad of vacation products and options offer mind-boggling choices. Do you choose an all-inclusive package, an escorted tour package, or do you go on your own . . . totally independent? Each travel choice has advantages and disadvantages.

Escorted Group Tours

Escorted group tours are vacation packages with a set itinerary for a pre-booked group of travelers. Local transportation, lodging, sightseeing, and some meals are included in the cost of the trip. Air travel to the destination may or may not be included. Local transportation is usually by motorcoach. Escorted tours may also include train or ship travel. The most significant differentiating factor is that a tour director from the tour operator or travel agency accompanies the travel group.

Advantages of an escorted group vacation package

- Accommodations, transportation, sightseeing and some meals are prearranged.

- You stay with the same group for the entire trip—get to know others.
- Peace of mind—the escort deals with problems that arise.
- A good way for a solo traveler to avoid being lonely and feel more secure.
- Good for exotic travel where independent travel may be difficult to plan/execute.
- Easier to budget—most expenses paid in advance.
- Save 15%–30% over an independent trip due to group buying power.

Disadvantages of an escorted group vacation package

- Not as much free time as desired.
- You stay with the same group . . . and may really get tired of them.
- You may not spend as much time as you would like at special attractions.
- "Down" time waiting for the group.
- Escorts may not be as knowledgeable or helpful as promised.
- Group meals tend to be "less than gourmet" quality.
- No opportunity for spontaneity—you have to go with the flow.

Independent Travel

With independent travel, there is no group, no fixed itinerary, no pre-arranged hotels, transportation, or guides . . . unless you arrange them yourself. Your travel options are wide open. You can go deluxe or on a budget or mix and match the two. You can plan everything ahead or "wing it" as you go along. (Winging it requires a free spirit, flexibility and fearlessness.)

Advantages of Independent Travel:

- You go where you want and do want you want . . . no strings attached.
- You meet a constant stream of new people.
- You can adjust your plans mid-trip.
- If you enjoy the planning process, it's more fun and challenging than having everything planned for you.
- You can stay in small, quaint places and dine in small, unique restaurants that can't accommodate large groups.

Disadvantages of Independent Travel:

- It may be difficult to find good deals without group buying power.
- It can be lonely and intimidating for non-extroverts.
- There's no help when there are problems.
- You may miss some sights and local history using a guidebook rather than an experienced tour guide.

Package Travel

Package travel is often a good compromise between an escorted group tour and independent travel. Travel packages have a fixed itinerary and include transportation and hotels, usually with a choice of meals and sightseeing options. There is no travel "group" other than sightseeing tours. You have as much free time as you wish. You control your expenses with a choice of pricing options and can take advantage of bulk tour pricing. You still have the convenience and security of planning assistance and some recourse when there are problems.

Package vacations are offered by tour operators, travel agents, and most major airlines

Travel Experience: **We travel all three ways. We traveled to Bali with an escorted small group (under 20) and enjoyed the convenience and security of having everything pre-arranged. We had an excellent escort and all local guides were knowledgeable and professional. On a recent trip to Hong Kong (another small escorted group) we were pleased with accommodations and amenities. The cost of the Hong Kong trip ($1088.00 per person for eight days) was less than our airfare alone would have been, going independent. On the contrary, on cruises, where most shore excursions involve forty or more people, we usually develop an aversion to the "herd" aspect after a few ports.**

Your choice depends on your travel personality and personal preferences. Ask yourself these questions:

1. **What is most important to me?** Some travelers like to see and do everything. They are ready and willing to be on the go from early morning until the wee hours. Others enjoy time to relax and savor the moment or spend an afternoon people-watching at a sidewalk café rather than trekking through every museum and cathedral in town. You may be a city-ite preferring the sights and sounds of a large metropolitan area to the serenity of nature or the exhilaration of outdoor adventure.

2. **Where do I fit in?** Are you more comfortable in a large group, with a few friends or alone? Do you prefer being with others of similar age and interests or do you like a diverse group? Do you like a casual atmosphere or a more formal one? Do you like to make decisions and solve

problems or do you want someone taking care of things for you?

3. **Is my budget realistic?** Do you want to travel in style or bare bones? How much are you willing to compromise to stay within budget?

Travel Homework: (Just for the *FUN* of it): Try the travel personality quiz on the website of the United States Tour Operators Association (USTOA). It's a quick 15-question multiple-choice test that provides interesting insights. You'll find it at www.ustoa.com. There's also a quiz to test your travel comfort zone and good information about tour operators and tour packages.

Meanwhile, let's assume you are interested in an escorted tour or vacation package. Researching travel tour packages is educational, enlightening and entertaining. Tour operator websites and brochures will stir your wanderlust and stimulate your travel dreams.

Once you decide on a destination or a couple of options, begin your research to find the right tour package. You have two excellent options for this research. Almost all major tour operators have websites and comprehensive brochures. Second, travel agents also offer a wide variety of brochures and professional guidance for finding the right package for you. Travel agents have access to tour packages and tours not available directly to the consumer online.

As you compile your tour package information, consider these aspects:

- **Understand exactly what is and is not included in the trip cost.** Compare type and location of accommodations, whether or not airfare to the destination is included, transfers to and from the airport, number of meals included, baggage handling and gratuities, services of an escort, single supplements, and taxes and other fees.

- **Compare tour company policies on deposits and cancellations.** Although policies appear similar, each tour operator has its own terms and conditions. Find out when and how initial deposits and final payments must be made. Be sure to note cancellation fees. Read the small print. If credit card payment is not an option, look elsewhere! (See *Chapter Four. Dollars & Sense.*)

  Will you be affected by currency fluctuations between the time you book your trip and the time for final payment? Get all services, terms/conditions and prices in writing. Don't judge a company by its website. Offers on the Internet are not offers in *writing*. According to the National Consumer League, offers on websites are not "policed" for accuracy and provide no proof for later claims.

  We repeat . . . the Internet is an incredible source of travel information and there are very credible online deals available, but buyer beware. It's easy to build a glitzy, flashy website. There is no guarantee that the company is what it appears. Before purchasing a tour package via the Internet, get all details in writing and check them out carefully.

- **Don't put off booking airfare.** If airfare is not included in your tour package, book your flight reservations before you confirm your tour package. A great tour package is no good if you can't get to the starting point. Compare the air add-on fare from the tour company to the fare you get directly from airline reservations or your travel agent. If you want to use frequent flyer mileage, your best chance is to plan at least six months in advance and be willing to go a day or more ahead of your trip or stay over afterward.

- **Invest in travel cancellation/medical insurance.** Your vacation tour/package is an important, and often expensive, investment. Protect it by spending a few dollars more for

travel insurance. (See **Chapter Four. Dollars & Sense.**)
Don't purchase travel insurance through the tour operator.
If the tour company ceases operation, your insurance may
also disappear.

- **Check out tour/travel companies carefully before you
  make an initial deposit**. Make sure the company is a
  member of a reputable travel organization such as United
  States Tour Operators Association (USTOA) or National
  Tour Association (NTA). Don't take the tour company's
  word for it. Check directly with USTOA or NTA via their
  websites or by telephone. Membership in USTOA requires
  a tour operator to be in business at least three years, have
  eighteen industry references, carry a minimum of $1
  million in liability insurance and provide $1 million in
  the form of a bond or letter of credit through the USTOA
  consumer protection plan in case of bankruptcy or default.
  NTA has similar requirements.

Most well-known and reliable tour operators have been in
business for many years. Some of these companies include:
**Abercrombie & Kent, Collette, Globus, Grand Circle,
Insight, Perillo, Pleasant Holidays, Tauck,** and **Trafalgar.**
We traveled to Hong Kong with Pleasant Holidays and we
were very pleased with every aspect of our trip. Friends and
family swear by Grand Circle and Trafalgar. Check out the
offers of these companies through their websites or brochures.

> **Travel Wisdom: A reminder! Watch out for claims that you have "won or been selected for a luxury vacation tour or cruise." This advertising come-on is a way to get you to pay for a trip that may or may not be legitimate. You may be told you have eighteen or twenty-four months to use your vacation after an initial "nominal" deposit or security payment. When you decide to take your bargain vacation, the company may be out of business or reservations may not be "available." Again, offers too good to be true are exactly that.**

Now, you've done your due diligence and booked an escorted group tour. Let's look at some ways to get the most pleasure out of your group travel experience.

- **Be realistic. Not everything will be perfect.** All travel involves compromise. You get what you pay for. On tour group pricing, don't be surprised if your hotel room faces the parking lot instead of the park. Don't expect gourmet group meals. If you are not paying luxury prices, don't expect champagne on a beer budget.
- **Give the escort a break.** Recognize that your escort is not a 24-hour-a-day companion. The escort is paid to be your liaison for local sightseeing, included meals, baggage services, and trouble-shooting problems. They are not paid to be at your beck and call for every little grievance, wish and command. Don't expect them to hold your hand every hour of the day . . . and night. Clarify the parameters of their role beforehand.
- **Give yourself a break.** Know when to say "whoa." If you hit your limit of togetherness, opt out. It's okay to say no . . . as long as it doesn't disrupt the tour for others. Skip a tour. Sleep in one morning and do your own thing. If you can't

stand the thought of another group dinner, go to the quaint corner café or order room service. Pay extra graciously. Tell the escort you won't be there so the group doesn't waste time waiting for you.

- **Make the effort to make new friends.** Add value to the tour for others and you will automatically make new friends. Greet everyone pleasantly each day. Introduce yourself and ask about their family, travels, or opinions. Buy occasional treats and share with the group. Offer to take photos of other travelers. (Hopefully they will reciprocate.) Share positive insights. Keep negatives to yourself. Don't knock everyone over to be the first person on or off the bus. Be on time. Don't keep the group waiting.
- **Don't be the group whiner.** On every tour there is a group whiner. The whiner always finds something wrong with everything. Sometimes they have to look hard, but don't worry . . . they'll find something to complain about. They are also the ones who seem to delight in keeping the group waiting while they shop a few more minutes or enjoy one more cigarette. Too bad the group can't vote them off . . . like the Survivor show!
- **Plan ahead.** Take along a daypack on all day tours. A backpack or tote bag is great for taking life's little comforts and necessities. Remember those Ziploc bags we're always talking about? They are perfect for packing a bottle of water, snack bar or piece of fruit, gum and mints. Add wet wipes, medications (headache meds, motion sickness remedy, antacids, Band-Aids, etc.) to your daypack. Don't forget sunshades and extra film or batteries. Toss in a book or magazine, travel journal and pen. Don't forget an international calling card to call home when time and chance permit.
- **Read books about your destination.** Buy a good travel book and highlight the "must see" places. Make notes in the margins as you see special sights or eat at recommended

restaurants. Add your recommendations and thoughts for future trips. (Or . . . a future travel book or article!) Look for a fiction or non-fiction book that takes place at your destination during a point in history. Imagine yourself in that venue.

- **Be alert for opportunities to make the memories last.** Don't waste time madly snapping dozens of photos from bus windows. They'll be blurred anyway. Pick special photo moments. Make notes in your travel journal—sights, sounds, and feelings you want to remember. Collect additional information about the sights that hold special interest. Shop with savvy. Choose souvenirs for yourself and others wisely. Long after the souvenir Eiffel Tower is tossed or sold at a garage sale, you will re-live pleasant memories when you decorate your Christmas tree with special travel ornaments. Add to special collections . . . start a collection.

Continue on for an excerpt from our travel journal. A trip to exotic Bali.

Christen's Travel Journal
Group Tour to Exotic Bali

Day One. Our tour group of sixteen people began our sojourn early morning out of Ft. Walton Beach. Over the next twenty-four hours we will fly to Atlanta, Newark, Amsterdam and into Singapore. The agony of so long in the air is eased by flying Singapore Airlines. Singapore Airlines turns out to be as good as we've always heard. The aircraft out of Newark is clean and comfortable. The flight attendants are professional, beautifully dressed, and actually friendly. Unlike most "cattle cars" the seats have more legroom than usual, footrests, adjustable head rests, and individual videos in each seat back.

Another pleasant surprise, we are served hot scented towels before the beverage service—in coach no less! All passengers are offered complimentary Piper Heidsieck Champagne. I could get used to this! Over the next eighteen hours on two flight legs we are offered numerous meals—actually good food. Passengers are provided with toiletry kits complete with toothbrushes, toothpaste, mouthwash, and other amenities.

Day Two. We arrive in Singapore early morning, bleary eyed and jet-lagged, but determined not to give in to sleep. We only have a day and a half here. Gotta see and do all we can.

Our travel group splits up to go separate ways. We take a harbor tour to get our first good view of Singapore from the water. The city and the harbor are incredibly clean. There is a boat operating in the harbor, patrolling and cleaning with a straining scooper on the front. There is no graffiti anywhere. There is no litter. In fact, we have been warned that there is a stiff fine for littering and jaywalking. We are careful to comply. (Chewing gum is a forbidden substance to bring into the country.)

After a delicious Asian lunch, still fighting fatigue, we hire a private car and driver for a quick land-based tour of the city. By late afternoon, we've had it. We succumb to a short nap. We have an early dinner and, with the help of Melatonin, a good night's sleep.

Day Three. I begin the day by almost setting fire to my hair. Instead of using the converter as I know I should, I just plug in hair dryer and curling iron and go for it. Flames shoot out of the hair dryer and my curling iron melts. Learned my lesson.

After a quick breakfast, we dash out to shop a little and then to Raffles Hotel for a world-famous Singapore Sling. Soon, it's time to go to the airport for our flight to Bali. We arrive in Bali very late evening. Before leaving the airport, we all become millionaires. Millionaires in Indonesian Rupiah . . . about $200.00 U.S.

We check in our hotel in Denpasar, Bali around midnight and crash. Tomorrow will be a full and fascinating day.

Day Four. May be the jet lag, but Hank and I awake very early and go exploring. Our hotel grounds are like a well-manicured tropical paradise. Heavy tropical vegetation and Hindu altars, like ancient ruins, throughout the grounds. It is very early. The air is fresh and heavy with the smells of exotic tropical flowers. There is no one else around. It's like our personal paradise. We walk down to the beach and stand on the edge of the South China Sea . . . almost on the exact opposite side of the world from home. This is our first *travel moment* on this trip.

After breakfast, our group assembles and we meet Bagush, our guide for the next few days. Traffic is heavy, but traffic here is predominantly motorbikes. There seem to be hundreds of motorbikes careening down the streets, laden with everything from ten-foot PVC pipes to huge baskets filled with produce, laundry, and everything imaginable. Our mini-bus negotiates the chaos well. We're glad we are not the driver. Bagush points out signs of the Hindu culture everywhere. There are statues to various gods in front of most homes and businesses. These gods wear "skirts" of black and white checked material. This pattern symbolizes the coexistence of good and evil in the world. There are also small offerings on the ground in front of businesses and homes. These offerings are fruit and flowers. We'll have to be careful not to step on one of them.

After a quick tour around Denpasar, we head into the countryside. One of our first stops is to see a traditional Barong Dance. The Barong is a creature who represents the positive spirit. He is a gorgeous creature who dances and struts his stuff with the help of two men inside. Soon, he is accosted by the evil witch, Rangda. Along with the supporting cast of

kings, princes, servants and a big monkey, a battle ensues. The
battle of good and evil. Good prevails and the Barong defeats
Rangda. I already know what my unique jewelry piece will be
here . . . got to have a silver Barong pendant!

Next we move on the Kintamani, and the rim of Mount
Batur, the island's large volcanic crater high up in the hills.
We enjoy a local lunch and shopping opportunities from very
aggressive vendors. Heavy-duty bargaining is the order of the
day. I purchase a great wood carving of an ancient fisherman
for our son for a mere $3.00. Now, the problem of how to get
it home. We also visit the Elephant Cave, which dates back
to the eleventh century as a place of worship. After stops
at several other temples and shrines and much walking and
climbing, we are ready for our stop for the night. And what a
stop!

We check into the Hotel Chedi in Ubud, Bali. In all
our travels, this hotel wins our vote as Best of the Best!
Accommodations are individual cottages with teakwood floors
and walls. Bowls of fresh orchids, candles and special snacks.
Private decks with chairs to enjoy the dense, cool, tropical
setting. And, then there is the bathroom. Right away we notice
there is no shower or tub in the elegant, huge, green marble
bath. There are doors leading out of the bath. Exiting, we find
a walled courtyard—a private rainforest—with a green marble
shower in the center. We took four showers over the next
twenty-four hours.

We walk down to the main house for dinner and enjoy our
meal outside, under a thatched roof, listening to a light tropical
rain fall and admiring the lush tropical surroundings. We could
stay here forever.

Day Five. Regretfully leaving the luxury of the Chedi, we
go deeper into the countryside. We see farmers plowing rice
paddies with oxen as they have for hundreds of years. Bagush
tells us their life expectancy is about thirty-seven years. We
decide we will never waste rice again. A visit to the Sangeh

Monkey Forest brings us up close and personal with these aggressive, but friendly, little creatures. Several other stops and some great shopping opportunities bring us to the end of the day and as the sun begins to set we are at the Tanah Lot Temple on the western shore of Bali. This temple, built literally in the sea, can only be reached at low tide. We enjoy cool beverages and watch the sky turn from shades of gold to red to purple as the sun drops into the sea.

The most exciting part of our evening is next. We climb a very steep path to the top of the cliffs to witness a traditional Monkey Dance. Performed by dozens of males ranging from children to the very old, this ancient dance is accompanied only by the haunting music of chanting human voices and performed by firelight in the deepening nightfall. We feel we have stepped right into the land of National Geographic. The perfect ending to our day. A real *travel moment*!

Following the ceremony, we carefully work our way back to the bus and head toward Denpasar for a much-needed night's rest. Tomorrow we have a free day to explore our surroundings in Denpasar.

Day Six. We awake refreshed and ready to go. We have already discovered that shopping here is an adventure in bargaining . . . and there are abundant bargains! We spend the morning in town and buy, buy and buy. This afternoon we treat ourselves to a massage. An example of bargains, a massage on the beach at our hotel is only $5.00 for thirty minutes. A bargain, but we opt for the massage in the hotel (air conditioned) spa lying on a table of silk peering through the opening at a stream running through the room with floating fragrant flowers. This luxury still only costs $20.00 for one hour.

Feeling pampered and mellow, we walk down to the beach for a sunset drink. As we again watch the sun slide into the sea, we decide this trip has been a continuous stream of *travel moments*. We are glad we are here . . . together.

Day Seven. Up early again, we take a morning flight to the island of Lombok. Few tourists visit Lombok, so we are as much of an attraction as the island and its inhabitants are to us. Our guide warns us that the natives are very curious about "white" people. They may want to touch us to see if the white comes off. They definitely do want to touch. I have on a loose-fitting top. Little hands try to lift it to see if I am the same color all over.

Hank's video camera almost causes a riot. As curious children want to get a look at the strange contraption, he flips out the side screen and shows a couple of young boys how they can see others in the screen. A crowd gathers to observe. Mothers bring babies to "see" them on camera. We enjoy the visit to the primitive village, but leave somewhat saddened at the living conditions.

As we board our bus, the children are begging, pointing with their fingers at their hands and pretending to write. Our guide tells us they are begging not for money but for pens or pencils for their school. We clean out our purses and wish we had brought along boxes of Bics.

We visit a wood carving factory and watch carvings being completed that tower ten feet or more. We visit a weaving factory and I get a chance to become a weaver. Strapped into a torturous contraption, I get a lesson in weaving the beautiful batik fabric . . . one thread at a time. The workers giggle at my clumsiness and shake their heads at my lack of talent.

Late afternoon finds us at our Lombok hotel. While clean and comfortable, this accommodation is not the luxury we have been treated to . . . yet it is one of the best hotels on the island. We notice another difference between Bali and Lombok right away. Lombok is predominantly Muslim and we hear the calls to prayer ringing throughout the island. We also do not feel welcomed here as we felt in Bali. We are glad we have seen Lombok, but somewhat relieved when we fly back to Bali the next day.

A short two weeks after our visit, we read in the news that Christians were being evacuated from Lombok due to hostilities.

Day Eight. We are back in our hotel in Denpasar for a final day before we begin the long, long trip home tomorrow. We treat ourselves to another massage and some last-minute shopping before an evening farewell dinner with our group.

Day Nine. We board a flight back to Singapore. Unfortunately due to flight schedules, we must spend about six hours in Singapore before the flight home. Some of our group go back into the city to shop. We decide to stay in the airport.

There is no airport in the world like the Singapore airport. It is more an experience than an airport. We sit in the main lobby, in a virtual indoor rainforest of towering palms, dozens of orchids and other exotic plants, beside a flowing stream and pond filled with the largest and most beautiful Koi we have ever seen. We are entertained by hourly concerts by pianists clad in tuxedos playing classics such as our favorite, Phantom of the Opera.

Gourmet dining is available at over a dozen restaurants. There is a hands-on interactive museum that enthralls adults and children alike. And, of course, there are shops and more shops. The six hours fly by and soon we are winging our way back to reality.

One of our favorite travel quotes describes this trip well.

We do not remember days, we remember moments.
                                                    - Cesare Pavese

CHAPTER TWELVE

SMOOTH SAILING

The voice of the sea speaks to the soul. The touch of the sea is sensuous, enfolding the body in its soft, close embrace.

- Kate Chopin

We admit it! We are prejudiced toward cruising . . . hooked on it. Here's why:

Twelve Best Things About Cruising

- Leave your worries behind at the dock; don't worry, no one will take them!
- Unpack only one time.
- Don't worry about where to eat . . . only how much!
- Visit exotic places without the hassle of multiple flights.
- Ideal vacation with children—especially teens. Quality family time is mixed with just the right degree of separation. Activities for everyone.
- Meet interesting fellow travelers from all over the world. Make lifelong friends.
- Escape ringing phones, stressful traffic, and demands of daily life.
- Do as much or as little as you choose . . . choose from dozens of activities.
- Enjoy an incredible variety of entertainment.

- Be pampered . . . and don't feel guilty about it!
- See spectacular sunsets and sunrises . . . and a starlit sky without the glare of city lights.
- Add it up! How many top resorts can you stay in, enjoy accommodations, a variety of excellent entertainment, gourmet meals, and constantly changing scenery for an average of $100 to $200 per day? Even with "hidden costs," cruising is a great travel value.

Convinced? Let's look a bit further at the joy of cruising.

Understanding Cruise Markets

Different cruise lines target different market segments. If you are budget conscious or have money to burn, there is a cruise for you. There are upscale lines catering to those demanding the finest, middle market lines, and budget lines offering a lively atmosphere at value prices.

Radisson, Seabourn, Silverseas and Crystal are four luxury cruise lines. Each of these lines offers gourmet food, elegant service, and many amenities. Cruise fares reflect this luxury approach and are significantly higher than value-oriented lines. But, don't rule out luxury cruising. If you are flexible and can sail on short notice, you can sometimes get a "great bargain" while lavishing in those luxuries. Visit their websites and examine the spotlight offers. Put your travel agent on alert for bargains.

Upscale mass market cruise lines deliver an excellent cruise experience below luxury rates. The majority of cruise lines are in this category. Princess, Holland America, and Celebrity are the top three players in this market. Again, check out their websites and special offers. Each cruise line has strengths and unique offerings.

For instance, one trademark Princess experience we always enjoy is Champagne Tower Night. Guests drink complimentary champagne, sample delicious crepes, and mingle with favorite crew members. You also get to try your hand at pouring champagne into the top glass and watch it cascade down over 700 glasses in a spectacular champagne tower. On Celebrity's Infinity, you can spend hours in a wonderful nature conservatory and learn the intricacies of floral arrangement. Holland America delivers service with genuine warmth that makes you feel like an old friend.

Toward the budget end of the mass market, Royal Caribbean, Norwegian and Carnival offer dining and entertainment experiences at surprisingly low costs—often less than $100 per day per person. There are few resorts or vacations you can enjoy at those prices. Again, each line has a distinctive personality. Royal Caribbean specializes in a unique variety of on-board lively experiences such as rock-climbing and ice skating. Carnival positions itself as the Fun Ships, attracts a younger party crowd, and offers great programs for families with young cruisers. Norwegian is best known for their free-style dining options.

Finally, there are specialty cruise lines that run the gamut from quiet elegant river cruises, to hands-on adventure cruises, to barefoot, sleep-on-deck casual cruises.

Variety is the spice of life. Study the differences and decide which cruise is right for your budget and lifestyle.

Choosing the Right Cruise and the Right Ship

This is another time when it's important to know your travel "personality" and be realistic about your travel budget. If you are a swinging single, you will be miserable on a cruise ship with seniors. (Generally the longer the cruise, the older the cruisers.) We have been among the oldest cruisers on a ship and among the youngest on another ship. Given the choice, we opt to be among the youngest at this stage in our lives.

Consider another personal choice. Do you want to stop at multiple destinations or have more sea days to relax onboard? We enjoy ports of call, but find it very tiring when there are almost daily stops. Sea days are good days to rejuvenate. We recommend at least two sea days on a seven-day cruise. Of course, the ultimate in sea days is a transatlantic or transpacific cruise. You will have five or six days to relax and enjoy all the ship has to offer.

Spend some time on the Internet. Research ships and itineraries. Check out the Sunday travel section of major newspapers, such as the *New York Times*, *Atlanta Journal*, or *Los Angeles Times*. One of the best websites for comprehensive cruise research is **www.cruisemates.com**. You'll find everything about the cruise experience, including cruise line and ship reviews. Call or visit your local travel agent and collect cruise brochures from several different cruise lines. An experienced travel agent can't be replaced. They know ships and will find the right cruise for you and your budget. A good travel agent saves you hundreds of dollars with special cruise promotions and upgrades.

Size and Age Matter

Ships carrying 1000 to 2000 passengers are considered "mid-sized" and those carrying over 2000 are "large." The "mega-ships" accommodate from 2500 to over 3600 passengers and are equivalent of a floating city or resort complex.

We've sailed on small ships with 700 passengers, mid-sized ships with 1700 and on the *Grand Princess* with 2600 passengers. All of these ships have advantages and drawbacks.

Large Ships
- Are usually newer, glitzier.
- Offer more numerous and more varied activities.

- Provide more dining options
- Have more public spaces.
- Handle rough seas better.
- Boast bigger casino/more shops.
- Offer large-scale, elaborate production shows.

Small Ships
- Have a more intimate feeling.
- Enjoy a more relaxing atmosphere, fewer activities.
- Service is more personalized.
- It's easier to get around the ship.
- Can get into ports or areas too small for large ships.
- Allow faster boarding and disembarking.

Often, it's not the *size* as much as the *age* of a ship that should influence your cruise choice. We prefer new ships. New ships have more affordable veranda/balcony cabins. Balcony cabins are very limited on older ships; consequently, they go for premium prices. New ships have the latest technology such as: Internet cafes, high-tech gym equipment, interactive game rooms, and sophisticated sound-and-light production shows. They have more public spaces, pools and spa facilities.

Although the cabins on many newer ships tend to be smaller, the soundproofing is much better. The room décor is updated and fresh. A small cabin seems larger with the open space of a verandah and sliding glass doors instead of a porthole.

On the opposite side, we've talked with fellow cruisers, especially senior travelers, who prefer the low key and classic ambiance of a small, older ship. It's important to know your personal preferences. No matter what your choice, there is a cruise for you!

Selecting the Right Cabin

Like ship size and age, the type of cabin you choose and its location in the ship are important cruise decisions that impact your travel budget and cruise enjoyment. Itineraries, budgets, and personal preferences determine the type of cabin you choose.

There are single, double, and triple/quad cabins. There are mini-suites, suites, and sometimes a penthouse suite. There are inside and outside cabins. There are cabins in the bow (front) and stern (back) of the ship and mid-ship. Some cabins are low in the ship; other cabins tower ten stories above the water at the top of the ship. So many choices!

On a short (less than a week) cruise, you may choose an oceanview cabin (window or porthole) or an inside cabin to save money. If you select an inside cabin, be sure you can handle being closed in with no window . . . no daylight in the cabin. Some travelers say inside cabins make them feel "snug and secure." And, you pay a lot less for an inside cabin.

On a long cruise (seven days or more) or scenic cruise (such as Alaska), we strongly recommend *spending more* and *getting much more*. A private balcony or mini-suite adds another dimension of enjoyment to your trip. If money is no object, go for that Penthouse Suite and live like the rich and famous!

Other than suites, think small. The average cruise ship cabin is about 180 square feet—that's the equivalent of a 10-ft x 18-ft. room. With twin beds or a queen-size bed, space is tight. The bathroom also has no wasted space. Cruise bathrooms are built for one person. If you choose a balcony cabin, the open space makes the cabin seem larger. If you have a triple/quad cabin, the third and fourth beds are drop-down bunks. Four people in a cabin get real cozy. We cruised with our sons several times sharing a room. Those cruises were *not* our most relaxing cruises . . . to say the least! If your budget can handle two cabins, especially with teenagers, go for adjoining rooms. You can keep a close eye on them, but not be too crowded.

Oceanview cabins and inside cabins are the same size cabin regardless of whether they are on a lower deck or high in the ship. As a rule, lower-deck cabins cost less. We prefer the high decks for the view. Many people prefer the lower deck cabins because they offer a smoother ride in rough seas.

There are other important location considerations. Before accepting a cabin assignment, look at a deck plan for the ship. Deck plans are available in cruise ships' brochures or online at most cruise ship websites. What is located above and below your cabin? What is on each side of your cabin? You don't want a cabin under the disco, show lounges, or the gym. You don't want a cabin next to the elevators, laundry, or equipment storage rooms. We usually avoid cabins next door to quad cabins. Four people in a confined space naturally make more noise. And, unless you want a stream of walkers and joggers parading past your window, avoid the Promenade Deck.

Cabins located in the mid-ship area are less influenced by the motion of the seas and have central access to all public areas of the ship. We're a little different in our approach. Our favorite cabin is in the stern (back) of the ship . . . preferably on a deck that opens out to a pool or hot tub. Cabins in the bow (the front) tend to catch the brunt of rough seas. As the ship hits each wave, it sounds like an explosion under your cabin.

Finally, when it comes to location, cruise representatives or travel agents may offer you a "guaranteed" cabin. A guaranteed cabin means no advance cabin assignment. Instead of an assigned cabin, you are guaranteed the best room available in your category with the strong possibility of being upgraded to a higher-category cabin. We avoid guarantees. There is *no* guarantee that the upgraded cabin is a desirable location. Go for the sure thing. Choose your cabin with care.

Later, if you are offered an upgrade, you can accept it or stay with your cabin choice.

Making Your Dining Choices

Requesting your evening meal seating is your next pre-cruise decision. Most of the time, your choice is between "first seating" at around 6 p.m. or "second seating" at about 8:30 p.m. There are advantages and disadvantages to both seatings. The 6 p.m. seating is very early for many cruisers. When you return to the ship from a late tour near sail-away time, you'll have to rush to dinner with no time to relax and unwind. If you enjoy a late afternoon nap or cocktails and snacks, the early seating is "too early." (We prefer the late seating rather than rushing to dinner after tours or a nap.) On the other hand, if you are traveling with small children or if you're accustomed to an early evening meal, you may prefer the first seating. Regardless of your seating choice, you won't miss any of the excellent evening entertainment. There are duplicate stage shows. On cruises with mature travelers, the early dinner seating fills up quickly. Request your preferred seating when you book your cruise . . . the earlier the better to get your dining choice.

On most ships you also have alternative dining options ranging from a casual buffet, to theme restaurants, to room service. You must plan ahead to sample alternative theme restaurants. Most require a reservation. We always check with the head waiter in the dining room early in the cruise to be sure we don't choose alternative dining on a special night, such as lobster or baked Alaska night. Try the theme restaurants one or two nights during the cruise. They offer a nice change of pace and unique entrée choices.

Next, request the type of table you prefer. There are tables for two, four, six, eight, and ten on most ships. Your dining enjoyment is enhanced or diminished by your table partners. We've had exceptionally compatible dinner mates . . . and some less than compatible ones. Nothing detracts from the enjoyment of a great meal and great service more than someone who complains about everything and can't be pleased.

We've found that the best odds for compatibility is a table for six. With a table for four, you are stuck if the other couple is not compatible. At a table for ten, service takes longer, it's difficult to talk across the large table, and probably one person or couple will not mesh with the group. If you are seated at a large table for eight or ten, alternate seats instead of taking the same seats night after night. By alternating seating, everyone sits next to a different tablemate each night and conversation is easier. (Hint: If there is a problem with your dining partners, the maitre'd can often arrange another table for you. Hopefully you are not the problem!)

Getting a Grip on Cruise Costs

First, don't let the prices in cruise brochures alarm you. Cruise fares listed in the back of a cruise line brochure are full price. Do your homework and you won't pay anywhere near that amount. Compare prices on cruise line websites and with cruise brokers. Ask your travel agent to research travel deals and find the best price for your dream cruise. If you've cruised with the same line before, ask about repeat cruiser discounts and upgrades. (The more you cruise with one line, the better the deals you are offered.)

The lead prices quoted in newspaper ads and specials on the Internet (the ones that say "from") are usually for an inside cabin deep in the bowels of the ship. No window. We've never sailed in an inside cabin. Lynne is claustrophobic and we enjoy opening the drapes each morning to new vistas. Once you sail with a veranda cabin, it's hard to go back. Verandahs are a luxury well worth the price difference. They offer a private retreat with all the benefits of being out on deck. On a scenic cruise, such as the Panama Canal, Alaska, or Greenland, a private balcony greatly enhances your cruise experience. We made a big mistake by cruising Alaska in an older ship with no veranda.

What else do you look for in pricing? Base cruise costs usually do **not** include port charges and government fees. These are fees that government/port authorities charge the cruise lines for docking facilities. Cruise lines naturally pass these fees on to the passengers. Port charges/taxes may add a hundred dollars or more to the overall cruise cost. Always ask if port charges are included in quotes.

Next, how will you get to the ship? There will be airfares and possibly accommodations charges if you're not within driving distance of the port.

Personal Experience: As a flight attendant, Lynne saw many unhappy passengers miss their ship because of airline delays. Consider adding a pre-cruise package. Fly in a day or two before the cruise. Enjoy your port departure city with the peace of mind that you will be at the dock to sail away!

Hidden Costs of Cruising

The major travel costs are included in your basic cruise fare. Be prepared for items not covered by your basic fare. On a recent cruise, a fellow passenger was shocked and embarrassed when, after she scooped up several shipboard photos and walked away, the photo shop associate chased her down and informed her there was a photo charge.

Here are some a la carte charges *not* included in your fare:

• Most cocktails, wine, beer and soft drinks. This includes the refreshments in the cabin mini-bar. There are usually one or two nights when cocktails are complimentary such as at the Captain's Cocktail Party. There are also daily drink specials.

Travel Wisdom: Cruise rules prohibit bringing your own liquor onboard. We have never had a problem bringing a bottle for personal consumption in our cabin. We pack it (in a plastic Ziploc bag in case of breakage) in our checked cabin luggage rather than in a carry-on. We also purchase six packs of soft drinks, mixes, and local wines in ports for cabin consumption. Coffee and tea are available in the casual buffet area at no charge.

- Spa and beauty services are pricey. Watch for specials, especially on port days when many passengers are ashore and business is slow.
- Ship's photos are great mementos. A ship's photographer is always around capturing cruise moments, including formal sittings. You don't have to purchase the photos, but the cruise line is betting you can't resist many personal photos. Photographs of attractions in ports are also offered. We usually purchase our initial embarkation photo and a couple of other special moments or port shots. Photographs usually cost between six to ten dollars.

Travel Wisdom: If your cruise involves a special occasion, such as a family reunion or wedding anniversary, a formal photo sitting is a great idea. When will the group be together again for a professional photograph? Purchase one 8x10 and take it to a photo center that offers color print copies. Copies are about $2.00 compared to $15.00 or more onboard ship. Makes a good travel memento for everyone

- Forget using ship-to-shore telephone for staying in touch with home. At $15 or more per minute, a few three-minute calls will zap your budget. Most cruise ships have Internet rooms. Internet usage ranges from a flat fee of $7.50 for fifteen minutes to a nominal fee for each email. Phone cards are also a bargain for calls when you are onshore. In the U.S., including Hawaii, cell phone coverage is good. Outside the U.S. you may want to rent an international cell phone for your trip.

> **Travel Wisdom: Set up a free email account with AOL, Yahoo or Hotmail before leaving on the cruise. I purchased a MailBug email station for my mother before a 15-day cruise. When we travel, we email her a brief travelogue daily and copy friends and family. Everyone loves it and we enjoy getting mail from home.**

- Expect charges for special activities such as trapshooting, golf simulators and interactive video games.
- Onboard ATM machines charge a fee of $5.00 or more per transaction. Your bank will also add their fee. Take the maximum allowable cash each time you use the ATM. to reduce the number of transactions. You can also cash personal or travelers checks at the Purser's Desk.
- Alternative restaurants typically charge a $3.00 to $20.00 service charge for dining. This charge covers the wait staff service. Alternative dining is usually worth the nominal cost.
- Cruise-operated excursions/tours add several hundred dollars to your shipboard account. You have several options. Most cruise lines send tour information with your initial package. You can get a good idea of what the tours include and the cost. Book appealing tours in advance. If advance booking is not available, book your tours as soon as you

get on board. Popular tours fill up fast. Another option is to research your destination on the Internet or with travel books and book a private tour or guide. We usually select ship excursions in some ports and opt for private guides in others. A third option is to wait until you disembark in port to hire a guide. Be careful booking tours in this way.

> **Travel Wisdom: There are some very good guides hanging around in port and some scam artists. If you are on a ship-operated tour and the bus breaks down, the ship waits for you. If you book a tour on your own and are late returning, you may "miss the boat!" Another problem with booking private guides in advance is the possibility that the ship's itinerary may change unexpectedly. All cruise lines reserve the right to cancel or change ports depending on the circumstances. If you pay a guide in advance and cannot contact him to cancel or change the booking, you will lose that money.**

- Tips are another significant shipboard expense. Most service employees on cruise lines earn **only** tips. Most cruise lines automatically add tips to your on-board account for your dining room wait staff and cabin attendant. Tips average about $3.50 *per day per person* for your table waiter and $1.75 per day per person for your assistant waiter. Cabin attendants get $3.50 per person per day. They work very hard for this money! There are also optional suggested tips for the head waiter and maitre'd. A 15% service charge is added to all drinks in lounges and bars.
- Gambling and bingo are popular cruise activities. If you're not careful, the casino and shipboard bingo will take a big chunk out of your discretionary funds. At $10.00 to $20.00 per session, sometimes with two sessions a day, playing Bingo adds a couple of hundred dollars to your account on

a seven-day cruise. Slot machines and gaming tables can escalate your debt from hundreds to thousands of dollars. We determine our bingo and slot budget in advance. If we win, great! If we lose, we know when to stop and consider the loss an entertainment cost.

All of these extra expenses are added to your shipboard account. At the beginning of your cruise you'll register a major credit charge card to settle your shipboard account. You will receive a shipboard card. This card identifies you and doubles as your cabin key. Guard it with care! Each time you present the card for a la carte services, the charge is added to your account. If you don't monitor them, it's easy for expenses to get out of hand. This is especially true when traveling with minors who have their "own" card. Develop a clear understanding of what and how much may be charged daily.

Travel Wisdom: Request from the purser's desk a printout of your charges to date about mid-point on the cruise. Keep tabs as you cruise and there'll be no surprises at the end of the cruise.

Don't let the extra charges deter you from cruising. Know what to expect. Budget for your extra cost activities . . . or just relax at your own pace and cut expenses.

What to Wear on a Cruise

Don't be intimidated when you look at the cruise brochures. You'll see glamorous couples decked out in formal wear or frolicking by the pool in designer swimwear. In reality, you will see a mixture of everything when it comes to cruise attire. Planning your cruise wardrobe is important.

First-time cruisers typically overpack. In defense against guests with six trunks for a seven-day cruise, cruise lines are imposing baggage restrictions per cabin. Don't panic.

Follow these guidelines and you'll be well equipped and well dressed. Your only excess pounds will be the ones you gain with all the wonderful cruise buffets!

- **Bears repeating: Don't overpack**. If you choose your attire wisely and pack smart, one large bag and one carry-on are enough for a seven to ten day cruise. (You will inevitably buy new things along the way!)
- **Formal nights (usually one to three nights on a seven to ten day cruise) require a tuxedo or dark suit for men and a short or long formal or semi-formal dress for women.** In our experience, about 50% of male cruisers wear a tux, 40% wear a dark suit or sports coat and tie, and 10% stand out from the crowd in leisure shirts. You can rent a tuxedo onboard if you wish. For female cruisers, a long or short elegant black dress goes anywhere. A striking brooch or beaded shawl can make the same dress look "new" for several wears. Black silk pants are cruise wear staple—easy to pair with several tops for a smart evening look. Finally, if you're "allergic" to formal attire, avoid it by choosing alternative dining such as the casual buffet, pizzeria, or room service on formal nights. Cruising is all about choices and opportunities!
- **For most casual evenings, opt for collared shirts and slacks for men and a sundress or nice pantsuit for women.** Dress like you are going to go to a casual, but nice, restaurant at home. Shorts are not allowed in the main dining room for dinner.
- **Bring an evening wrap**. Show lounges and the dining rooms can be chilly. Since evening wear is often bare-shouldered, a classic black silk or beaded shawl is an elegant touch.

- **Daytime wear runs the gamut from funky to fabulous . . . tacky to terrific.** You'll see a bit of everything among your fellow cruisers. (We've promised each other that Hank will never wear plaid Bermudas with a striped shirt and black socks with sandals and I will never wear gold lame' from head to foot.) Cruises are a great chance to show off pretty sundresses or tropical print shorts or slacks sets. Start with several pairs of shorts, slacks and tops in coordinated colors to mix and match. Don't load your bag down with t-shirts. Buy some great destination shirts along the way.

   Choose easy-care clothing. Take advantage of washable lightweight knits that can be washed and hung on the shower clothesline and require no ironing. (Don't pack an iron! There are irons and ironing boards in the ship laundry room. On the same note, leave the hairdryer at home. Every ship we've sailed on has had a cabin hairdryer.) Overall, think comfortable, casual and smart. Plan your cruise attire by sticking to the basics discussed in *Chapter Two-- Packing Smart*

- **Swimsuits with pockets can double as shorts for men.** Take two swimsuits. You won't have to don a wet suit, if you decide after a morning swim to jump in the spa in the afternoon. Swimwear cover-ups are required in interior public areas of the ship. For maximum use, choose a cover-up, like a sarong, that doubles as casual wear. Don't forget a hat (for both men and women) and a pair of snappy sandals.

- **Skip the bathrobe.** Enjoy the luxury of fluffy terry robes provided by the cruise line. You probably can't resist purchasing one to take home. If there is no robe in your cabin, ask your attendant for one. If the cruise line doesn't provide a robe, let your swimwear cover-up double as a sleep robe.

- **When cruising in a cold climate, think layers rather than bulk.** Pack silk long johns, medium-weight knits and a good windproof, waterproof jacket. Gore-Tex jackets can't be beat. Don't forget a warm knit hat and gloves. We made that mistake on an Alaska cruise and paid $30.00 for a set that cost $3.00 at Wal-Mart.

Travel Experience: On one of our fifteen-day cruises, we arrived for dinner to find two mature women waiting outside the dining room for us. One of them said, "Honey . . . we wait for you every night to see what ya' have on. Ya' got it!" It was a supreme compliment to packing well! I wasn't dressed in Versace . . . just simple elegance with unique accessories. Total outfit including accessories: under $50.00. Sure made my day!

Travel Wisdom: Always be on the lookout for unique and inexpensive accessories, such as jewelry, scarves, belts, etc. When you spot a special piece, grab it. Add it to your travel attire inventory. Stand out from the crowd. Use creative touches. Look good. Feel good. And, bask in the compliments.

Setting Sail

The big day is finally here! The most jaded cruisers get excited when they see that big beautiful ship sitting at the dock. Stepping aboard is a special moment on every cruise. Passengers who enjoy a cruise the most are those open to new experiences. New experiences include meeting new people (both fellow travelers and crewmembers), trying new foods, and participating in cruise activities. Getting the most out of your cruise requires an open mind, flexibility, and a healthy sense of humor. (If you used our packing checklist, you brought all three of these traits along!)

It takes several hours for your luggage to be delivered to your cabin. Use this time to get acquainted with the ship. Pick up the ship map in your cabin and go exploring. Enjoy the sail-away "drink of the day" and indulge in the buffet for early boarders.

We use this initial reconnaissance to discover favorite spots for relaxing on deck and to establish our emergency meeting points (See **Chapter Five, Travel Health and Safety**). You are also required to participate in a lifeboat drill shortly before departure. Pay attention and follow crew instructions.

Soon, it's time for the Sail Away Party. Get out on deck with everyone and experience the thrill of watching the lines cast off as your ship leaves the dock. Leave your worries at the dock. (Don't worry. No one will take them . . . they'll be waiting when you return.) Relax and prepare to be pampered and entertained.

Each night the ship's official newspaper is delivered to your cabin. This daily ship news tells you what activities are planned for the following day, what is "on sale" in the shops, what time the ship arrives and departs from ports of call, and a list of dining opportunities. It's fun to plan the next day's activities. For example:

25 Things to Do on a Day at Sea

1. Sleep in and enjoy wake-up coffee on your private verandah.
2. Go for an early morning walk or jog around the deck.
3. Enjoy a sit-down four-course breakfast, a bountiful buffet on deck, or private breakfast on your veranda.
4. Read a good book in the sun.
5. Attend a cooking class, ice-carving demo, or tour the galley and be amazed by shipboard efficiency.

6. Get educated. Almost all ships have onboard guest lecturers on a wide variety of topics.
7. Take a dance or yoga class.
8. Go to a movie.
9. Play the slots/tables in the casino.
10. Attend an art auction (free champagne!)
11. Shop the ship's stores.
12. Enjoy afternoon high tea.
13. Get a massage.
14. Play bingo.
15. Participate in shipboard games, from trivia to shuffleboard.
16. Learn more about wines at the wine tasting.
17. Practice your golf swing . . . or trap shooting.
18. Go to the game room and strike up a game of bridge or checkers.
19. Introduce yourself to a fellow cruiser and chat.
20. Watch an incredible sunset.
21. Workout in the gym.
22. Go for a swim or relax in the spa.
23. Make love.
24. Daydream as you gaze at the ship's wake.
25. Eat, eat & eat again.

Get the picture? You will not be bored!

All too soon . . . it's the last day of your cruise. Where did the time go? Time to pack your bags again. Packing is easier this time. No worries about wrinkles and what to take.

Biggest problem . . . getting all the souvenirs and purchases home. Remember the collapsible bag you packed in the bottom of your luggage? You'll be glad you have it. The cruise shop also has an "overflow" bag on sale during the last few days of the cruise. (Smart on their part, sales are always brisk!)

Pack your important "can't lose" or breakable items in the collapsible bag. Don't forget medications and a change of clothes. The collapsible bag becomes your carry-on bag and the original carry-on bag gets filled with dirty clothes and checked with other luggage. Attend the disembarkation talk to learn how to expedite customs/immigration clearance.

You will receive color-coded baggage tags. These tags are for identification and indicate the order for disembarking. Checked baggage must be tagged and outside your cabin door by midnight.

Travel Wisdom: Very important tip! In addition to your carry-on bag, be sure to keep clothes to wear in the morning. You don't want to parade off the ship in your pajamas! It happens!

The morning of disembarkation, you must vacate your cabin immediately after breakfast. (The crew has only a few hours to get ready for the next 1000-3000 passengers.) Count on spending two to three hours in one of the ship's public areas while customs clears the ship. Be patient. Read a good book. Reminisce about the cruise. Plan your next cruise. Your time will come. Waiting is a good time to check your customs form and make sure it is complete and correct. Be absolutely certain you are not bringing home any restricted items that will delay your progress through customs.

Back to disembarking, when your color code is called, exit the ship. Claim your luggage and clear customs. Again, be patient. There are lines for immigration and customs. Don't make jokes or complain. Their work is serious and customs officials are not known for their sense of humor.

Personal Experience: Take a Lesson from Lynne. We were flying to New York returning from a wonderful cruise that terminated in Barcelona. In the Barcelona airport, I purchased an incredible huge string of fresh garlic. It was supposedly "approved for import into the United States." I tied it to the outside of our carry-on luggage and declared it on the customs form. On arrival in customs, the official took one look at that garlic and ordered us to the Agricultural Area . . . with all of our luggage. For the next two hours, we had to unpack all our bags to prove we were not bringing in other "forbidden fruit." The string of garlic was destroyed as possibly harboring Mediterranean fruit fly. We missed our connecting flight and were delayed several hours waiting for another one. Being an experienced traveler, after all those years as a flight attendant, I learned this lesson the hard way! (Hank has never let me live this down!)

Suffice it to say, disembarking is not as much fun as embarking! Soon, you'll be home telling everyone about your wonderful cruise and planning the next one!

O'er the glad *waters* of the dark blue sea, Our thoughts as boundless, and our souls as free."

- Lord Byron

Continue on for an excerpt from our travel journal . . .
Cruising the Med.

CHRISTEN'S TRAVEL JOURNAL
SAILING THE MED . . .

Day One. Venice, Italy

After a long night flying, we arrive at the airport in Venice.
It is a welcome sight to exit baggage claim and see the cruise
representatives holding welcome signs. Worth the transfer
charge not to have to fend for ourselves. We claim our bags
(breathing a sigh of surprise and relief when they are actually
there) and board the bus for the pier.

The first sight of the *Golden Princess* is breathtaking. She
sits in her berth, gleaming white in the sunshine, towering
sixteen stories over the city. We deposit our carry-on bags in
our cabin and venture out on our verandah for our first view
of the city. Although jet lag is creeping up on us, we decide to
fight it and not waste a minute of our visit to Venice. We take
a *vaporetto* (water bus) from the pier into the heart of the city.

The pace, though bustling, is noticeably quieter and more
relaxed than in other major cities. Could be the absence of
automobiles, buses, and motorbikes. No traffic jams, blaring
horns, squealing tires, and noxious exhaust fumes.

The center of the city is St. Mark's Square. It is alive with
sights and sounds. We hear the bells of the Campanile Tower
at half past the hour. A symphony of the past. Everywhere
small children and some adventurous adults feed and chase
the thousands of pigeons of St Marks, which almost seem to
outnumber the people. This is a wonderful place for people
watching. Groups of teens amble by with multi-colored hair
and avant garde attire. Old men and women stroll arm in arm.
Young couples and not-so-young couples steal kisses as they
glide in gondolas through the canals and under the bridges.

Strolling violinists entertain. Vendors with colorful wares are set up along the sidewalks. And, of course, the tourists are not hard to pick out clad in their shorts and t-shirts. (American tourists are the only people you see in shorts in most countries in the world.)

We browse the shopping kiosks and enjoy a glass of wine at one of the many sidewalk cafes. Jet lag is catching up and we decide it's time to take the water taxi back to the ship for a nap. After a nap, we unpack and enjoy a drink on deck, watching night fall on Venice.

Day Two. Venice

After a good night's sleep we are almost good as new. We really enjoy overnight on the ship in port. Ready for another day in Venice, we set off on a shore excursion to visit the Murano Glass Factory and experience more of the flavor of Venice.

Arriving at the glass factory, we have the opportunity to see the glassblowers in action. After admiring Murano glass for years, we decide to browse a bit for the perfect memento of our visit. After we splurge on a Murano fish in the "upstairs" showroom we were escorted to, we discover the real bargains are actually in the "basement" you pass through as you exit the factory. Of course, there we find the perfect piece, a beautiful gondola in deep blues and green and a bunch of grapes in deep greens and purples for under $25.00. We purchase them and remind ourselves that we need to be more careful about practicing what we preach in **Travel Wisdom** when it comes to shopping savvy.

Back to the water bus, for a visit to the San Giorgio cathedral and a much-awaited gondola ride. We settle into our seats in the gondola and our handsome young gondolier clad in the traditional black pants, striped shirt and straw hat guides us away from the dock.

Time seems to stand still as we slip silently through the deep green waters of the maze of canals. We pass homes where the garage houses a small boat instead of the usual car. Window boxes are filled with bright geraniums. Freshly laundered colorful clothing hangs from balcony clotheslines. The only sounds seem to be the coos of the pigeons, beautiful bells of the bell tower, and occasional warnings sung out from gondoliers approaching sharp turns in the canals. Gondolas and motorized water taxis slide past each other with inches to spare. What a wonderful way to spend a morning hour.

We return to the dock and stroll the labyrinth of alleyways with interesting shops and cafes we saw during our gondola ride. As we wander deeper into the inner city via the alleyways and over canal bridges, we are surrounded by the sights and smells of Venice. Smells of fresh garlic and herbs from the cafes, freshly baked bread from bakeries, the perfume of the fresh flower stalls, and the pungent smell of leather from shops stacked with jackets, handbags and luggage.

A sidewalk café calls to us. We spend the next hour savoring pasta in garlic and olive oil, gourmet Italian cheeses, a platter of *frito misto* (tiny fried fish) and linger over a bottle of Proscecco (a refreshing sparkling wine). We decide this is a special *travel moment.*

Finally, it's time to return to the ship for sail away. One of the best things about cruising is unpacking your bags one time and relaxing at the end of a busy sightseeing day as your "home away from home" sails on to another exotic destination with new adventures waiting.

We sip champagne on our cabin verandah as we sail out of Venice. We hear the strains of the wonderful song "*Con Te Partiro*" . . . "Time to Say Goodbye". The bell tower chimes the six o'clock hour. This is a perfect way to say goodbye to a remarkable city bathed in late afternoon sunlight and caressed by warm Mediterranean breezes. We are already planning a return visit . . . someday.

Days Three and Four. Relaxing at Sea

A day at sea is a day all about choices. Choices begin on awakening. Enjoy a leisurely breakfast on your private verandah or indulge in a bountiful breakfast at the top of the ship. Choices. Relax in the sun beside one of five pools. We choose the highest deck overlooking the endless wake of the ship. Play poolside games or try your luck at bingo or in the casino. Attend a port lecture or a self-improvement lecture. Have a mid-morning snack and work off calories in the state-of-the-art gym.

Choices. Lunch time rolls around. Go to the dining room for a sit-down five-course lunch. Back to the buffet on deck. Nothing is as good as a hamburger grilled in the open air at sea. Or . . . maybe a specialty pizza and a cold beer?

Choices. After lunch, a nap on deck. Attend a cooking class or wine tasting. Get a massage or facial. Bid on art work while sipping complimentary champagne. Try your hand at table tennis, shuffleboard, high-tech interactive games or work on your golf drive. See a first-run movie. Make new friends in the card/game room. Go for a swim . . . and so on and on.

Choices. All too soon, the day winds down. Watch an incredible sunset. There is no sunset like a sunset at sea with no land in view. As the sun sinks into the sea, golden, red, and plum colors fill the sky and sea. A wonderful time at sea. After sunset, we go to the cabin for a nap before dinner. When at home would you ever take a nap right before dinner?

Evening choices. The ship comes alive at night with entertainment in over a dozen clubs including a Las Vegas-style production show in the main theatre. Choices. Dress for dinner in the main dining room, a seven-course meal with interesting conversation with your tablemates. Opt for a romantic dinner for two at one of the specialty restaurants on board. Stay in your swimsuit and dig into the buffet on deck. Have room service.

Tonight, we choose Sabatini's, the Italian restaurant. Gabrino, our server, brings an extensive menu. Then, he tells us not to order any appetizers; he'll be bringing them all! Twelve wonderful samples, ranging from marinated porcini mushrooms, cheeses, shrimp, oysters, artichokes, caviar, and more. He reminds us to pace ourselves, there is much more to come. Between courses, we sip a smooth Merlot and relive our Venice adventures. Next is a seafood cioppino soup, followed by a Caesar salad. Three pastas roll out . . . yes, three. We are slowing down, but sample each. Finally, the entrée. lobster tails. And, there's still dessert. A tray appears with delectable choices, tiramusi, meringues, cheesecake, cannoli, and, marzipan.

Choices: The evening production show, a visit to the casino, a quiet after-dinner drink in one of the clubs, dancing in the disco sixteen stories over the sea. We decide on a walk around the promenade deck to savor the sea air . . . and maybe walk off a few of the million calories we consumed at dinner. After a quick visit to the Internet café to email home, we enjoy a Tribute to Broadway production show. Before turning in, we spend a few minutes on our verandah in awe of the evening sky. With no city lights, we are awed by the beauty of an endless sky filled with stars like glittering diamonds and a sea bathed in the light of a full moon.

The next day, another day at sea, is a repeat of the first . . . with more choices.

Day Five. Istanbul, Turkey

Why would anyone on vacation get up before sunrise? To see the once-in-a-lifetime view of a spectacular sunrise over the Bosporus Straits and not miss one minute of the approach into Istanbul. Up until a week ago, we didn't think this would be a port of call for our trip. With the war in Iraq, Turkey had been under a travel warning and the stop was changed. Fortunately, things are going well and with the travel warning lifted, we are looking forward to this historic city, the seat of multiple civilizations.

Not knowing exactly what to expect in the way of a welcome for Americans, we elect to take an escorted shore excursion. Our Turkish guide, Hayat, speaks perfect English and assures us we are "dear guests" of the Turkish people. We see the Hippodrome, the enormous stadium area used for chariot races. The Blue Mosque with its 20,000+ delicate blue tiles and seven towering minarets. At St. Sophia's Mosque, we encounter large groups of school children. They regale us with cheerful smiles, waves, and shouts of "Hello, Hello." Our guide tells us they are not asking for anything except a Hello or Good Morning in return. They want to go home and tell their parents that they saw Americans and spoke English to them. They are beautiful.

We move on to the Grand Bazaar. A shopper's paradise of over four thousand market stalls spread over sixty-five indoor streets. It is overwhelming. I need more time! Making the best of limited time, we bargain for meerschaum pipes, intricately woven belts, beautiful blue "Eye of God" bracelets, and other special treasures. Fellow travelers purchase Turkish carpets at bargain prices. Bargaining is the order of the day. The merchant states his price. We offer 50% of the asking price and usually end up paying about 60% of the original asking price. Unlike markets in other countries, where bargaining and haranguing become unpleasant, the Turks bargain with a smile and offer herbal tea to their shopping guests. All too soon it's time to return to the ship. We vow to come back to Istanbul someday!

As the *Golden Princess* sails away at sunset, we hear the Muslim call to prayer echoing throughout the city and the mosques with their towering minarets no longer seem so strange and unsettling.

Day Six. Kusadasi, Turkey

Kusadasi is a small seaport village. It is the gateway to the ancient ruins of Ephesus, the home of the Virgin Mary. As we sail into the sheltered harbor of Kusadasi at noon, we are surrounded by an emerald green sea, rolling hills, and a sense of timelessness. We decide not to take a ship's tour, but to visit the village and enjoy a leisurely Turkish lunch at one of the charming seaside cafes. We make our choice for dining and are greeted by the proprietor as if we are guests in his home.

As we sit at our seaside table, literally in the shadow of our ship, we recognize another *travel moment*. Our host brings us a dazzling array of salads from the sea, Turkish style. We sample octopus salad, lobster salad, squid, cheese-stuffed phyllo pastries, and other dishes we can't identify, but find appetizing and delightful. Next the host brings out a large sea bass, still flapping and breathing, to show us the freshness. We watch as it is grilled and served atop roasted eggplant and peppers. Topped off by a bottle of Dulca, the local Turkish wine, this is a meal to remember.

We spend the afternoon wandering the narrow streets and shopping the markets of Kusadasi . . . which we find much more rustic than the Grand Bazaar, but equally filled with bargains. We buy saffron for everyone in our cooking club at home for about $2.00 per bag.

We notice the streets of Kusadasi have blue stones with the Eye of God set into the cobblestones. We are told these Eyes of God are symbolic of protection. We buy a dozen to take home as gifts. One of the most beautiful ones hangs in my office window and I enjoy looking at it as I work at my desk. We sail away at sunset as the hills are bathed in the last golden hues of day.

Day Seven. Athens, Greece

We awake to find we are already docked at the pier in Athens. Not a particularly scenic location. We meet our tour group and motor away from the pier. Immediately we are assaulted with the horrendous traffic and noise of Athens. As we wind slowly through congested city streets we see construction underway for the 2004 Olympics. Although the setting is perfect—the origin of the games—we shudder to think about the modern-day traffic problems compounded by thousands more visitors.

We finally reach the area of the Acropolis, along with dozens of other packed tour buses and throngs of school children. Seeing the Acropolis has been on my lifetime to-do list for many years. I am determined to brave the masses and climb to the top to stand outside the Parthenon and Temple of Athena. The crowds prove to be only part of the problem. No sooner than we reach the top of the steep uphill climb and wait in line to push through the single opening into the Acropolis, the skies open up. Thunder, lightning and a downpour send the thousands of visitors scrambling back through the small entrance. There is nowhere to get out of the rain. It seems the gods (particularly Zeus, Lord of the Sky) are trying to tell us something.

To make things worse, we again violated our own advice. Our rain ponchos and umbrella are tucked safely in our day travel bag on the bus! We are soaked.

After a brief look around and a couple of quick photos, we join the masses pushing and shoving to get down the hill and out of the rain. It is actually a dangerous situation. This is definitely not what I envisioned when I read up on Greek mythology prior to the tour. Working our way back to the bus, we purchase cheap t-shirts so we can shed our wet shirts.

After the friendliness and warmth of the Turks, the Greeks do not seem very friendly or happy. Our guide confirms that Greeks simply do not smile a lot . . . at least not until after 9 P.M. when the *ouzo* (potent Greek liquor) kicks in. We could use some *ouzo* right now!

We again fight traffic to the Plaka shopping area. After buying traditional worry beads, we are ready for a Greek lunch at a quaint outdoor café. (The rain has stopped.) Here, we are not disappointed. We feast on Greek wine, eggplant, moussaka, and a sampling of appetizers.

We realize once again days like today are the reason we love cruises. We are glad not to be spending several days in the congestion and chaos of Athens. We came, we saw, and we are ready to move on.

Day Eight. Another Day at Sea

After a hectic day in Athens yesterday, and several ports in a row, a day at sea is a welcome respite. All those choices again. "Life just doesn't get any better than this!"

Day Nine. Naples and Pompeii

Situated in the shadow of Mt. Vesuvius, the Bay of Naples offers a scenic harbor for cruise ships. Since I was there over thirty years ago, I have looked forward to returning to Pompeii and seeing it with Hank. We decide to get brave and take a "physical" tour that includes climbing to the rim of the volcano. After a quick breakfast on deck, we meet our shore excursion group on the pier and set off for a scenic drive that will take us part of the way to the top of Mt. Vesuvius. Our guide is a double for Al Pacino in looks, voice, and mannerisms, and he relishes the role. This is going to be an entertaining trip!

The drive up Vesuvius *is* scenic and harrowing, with one hairpin turn after the other and sheer cliffs on each side. The roads are narrow so when we meet other tour buses or automobiles, one or the other must back up and pull as far to the side as possible to allow the other to pass. Thanks to the expertise of our driver, we arrive at the walking point alive and intact. We are provided with walking sticks and at first we decline them, but accept them after returning climbers tell us they are a necessity.

The climb from here to the rim of Mt. Vesuvius takes about thirty minutes, straight uphill on a sand-and-gravel trail that tends to shift underfoot. We are grateful for our walking sticks. Near the top, we realize we are not in as good shape as we thought. It is humiliating to be passed by fellow travelers fifteen years older than us. We are both huffing and puffing but continue our climb.

The climb is worth the effort. As we peer into the crater of Mt. Vesuvius our guide tells us that historically the volcano erupts every fifty years. It has not erupted since 1949. It is overdue. Although there is greenery growing in the crater and it looks very benign, we notice steam coming out of fissures around the sides of the crater—a sure sign there is activity somewhere in the depths underneath.

The trek downhill is easier than going up and we arrive back at our bus on time. The drive down Mt. Vesuvius is as harrowing as going up . . . maybe more so. But we survive and move on to Pompeii.

As we enter the gates of the ancient civilization, we can almost hear the chariots rambling down the cobblestoned street and visualize the wealthy citizens going about their daily lives. Pompeii was a very advanced and prosperous civilization when disaster struck on an August day in 79 AD around 11 a.m. We stand in the antiquarium area with Vesuvius looming in the background eight miles away. We imagine the terror as the ground began to shake and in 102 seconds the thunderous eruption buried Pompeii under twenty feet of ash and cinders. Civilization ceased. Walking the streets of Pompeii, with a knowledgeable guide, is a fascinating experience. Seeing plaster cast bodies of citizens caught in their final moments of life is chilling. All the while, Mt. Vesuvius sits in the background, seeming benign, a constant reminder of how quickly life can change.

We return to the ship for sail away. As we enjoy our evening drink sailing out of the Bay of Naples, we toast Mt. Vesuvius and wish those well who dwell in her shadow.

Day Ten. Livorno, Italy

Livorno is the port city for excursions to Pisa and Florence. Since we have toured both cities on a previous cruise, we decide to spend part of a leisurely day in Livorno and then return to the ship for a quiet afternoon by the pool. The port of Livorno is not a scenic location and is very obviously a working seaport. Our view is of cranes, freighters, and row upon row of shipping containers.

We enjoy a late breakfast and take our time getting off the ship. Taking the shuttle into the center of the city, we stroll through the local market place. This is not tourist shopping territory. It is a local produce market crowded with housewives doing their morning produce shopping. The stalls are filled with wonderful fruits, vegetables and flowers . . . a riot of color and appeal. We move on to an indoor marketplace with stalls that run the gourmet gamut. There are pasta shops with fresh pasta of every imaginable variety hanging in the window. Meat shops abound with pungent smells of *proscuitto* and *pancetta*. The sweet smell of sugar drifts from colorful candy shops and bakeries. The aroma of fresh coffee competes with the aroma of fresh herbs. Olive shops call to Hank with dozens of jars of specialty olives, capers, and fresh garlic. This "grocery" store is unique and we want to buy some of everything to take home. Hank reminds me of the "Garlic Disaster" when I attempted to bring garlic back from Barcelona on a previous cruise and got busted by Agriculture. We refrain from purchasing but decide to return to Italy in the near future for a culinary tour.

Returning to the ship, we have a late lunch and relax by the pool with a good book. We both enjoy quiet time on the ship when it is in port and the majority of the passengers are off touring. At sunset, we sail for Monte Carlo.

Day Eleven. Monte Carlo, Monaco

Sailing into Monte Carlo is entering the world of the "Rich 'n' Famous." Our ship is surrounded by sleek yachts that look like ships themselves. One of the largest, docked near us, has a helicopter on the aft deck and launches a thirty-six-foot "runabout" to go into the city. Monte Carlo is getting ready for the Grand Prix in just a few days. It is a scene of frantic activity. Difficult to walk around and enjoy the colorful street since bleachers and media trucks fill virtually every street. We are disappointed that we can't sit at a sidewalk café and watch the beautiful people stroll by. The only thing we see is the backside of bleacher seating. We decide the view is better from the ship and return to relax and watch the yachts glide in and out of the harbor. Rain moves in for the afternoon and we take advantage of this time to begin packing for the return home.

Day Eleven. Barcelona, Spain

One of our favorite cities. Since we were here on a previous cruise, we again forgo tours and spend the day rambling along La Rambla, the famous pedestrian street that stretches almost a mile through the heart of the dining and shopping district. All sides of La Rambla are lined with outdoor cafes serving delectable varieties of *tapas*, small appetizers limited only by imagination. We stop at several cafes and try their specialties with chilled sangria. Like New Orleans, there are street entertainers on every corner. We watch magicians; musicians and muses mesmerize the crowds. After a little shopping . . . and more sangria and tapas . . . we return to the ship for our last night onboard.

Day Twelve. Homeward Bound

Way too early, we disembark, say goodbye to the *Golden Princess*, and head for the airport to begin the long trek home. We will fly to Paris and connect to Atlanta and then Ft. Walton Beach. We use the long flight from Paris to Atlanta to recap our memories and begin planning our next cruise. Tahiti? Australia? Or, maybe, Beijing!

CHAPTER THIRTEEN

AIRS ABOVE THE GROUND

To most people the sky is the limit. To those who love aviation, the sky is home.

— Unknown

The year was 1965 . . . or maybe it was 1970 . . . or 1975. Airline travel was special. Passengers dressed up to travel by air. Stewardesses/stewards served meals on virtually every flight over one hour. They greeted passengers at the door and assisted them in stowing their bags. They passed out magazines, pillows and blankets. They chatted with passengers and smiled . . . a lot! Flying was something to look forward to.

That was over twenty-five years ago. Before. Before airline deregulation. Before overcrowded flights and overcrowded skies. Before September 11, 2001.

All I ever wanted to be was a flight attendant. I was so fortunate to live my dream for over twenty years when air travel was at a peak of graciousness and glamour. Today, it makes me sad to hear passengers complain about almost every aspect of flying. From business travelers to seniors to families, passengers dread the thought of "having" to fly, rather than delighting in the thrill of air travel. I can't bring back the good ole' days, but hopefully this chapter will help reduce the stress and strain of air travel . . . and maybe put some fun back into the sky.

Finding a Flight

Whether you want to see the harbor in Hong Kong, dive the Great Barrier Reef or visit Aunt Susie in Topeka, you gotta find a flight. And, you have three choices for booking an airline flight. One: Call airline reservations. Two: Book a flight over the Internet. Three: Use the services of a travel agent. Regardless of which way you choose to book your flight, if you want the best deal, there are two "musts."

1.Plan ahead. We've repeated this litany throughout *Travel Wisdom.* Spontaneity is a wonderful thing . . . except when it comes to booking air travel. If it's Tuesday and, on a whim, you decide to hop out to San Francisco for a couple of days. You will pay dearly for this whim. Best routing, best fares, and best seat choices must be purchased at least fourteen to twenty-one days in advance. Best fares usually require a Saturday night stay. Best airline deals also require flexibility. If you adjust your travel days forward or backward a day or so, or fly out of an alternate airport, you have more choices. Travel during a holiday period requires even more advance planning and flexibility.

Travel Wisdom: There is one exception to booking in advance. In the event of a death in the immediate family, most airlines offer a special bereavement fare (usually 50% off full fare pricing) and remove fare restrictions. You need proof of death such as a letter from a physician or a death certificate.

---

2. Do your homework. The Internet provides a wealth of information (sometimes too much) for travel research. You can:
- Research flight schedules and prices.
- Uncover special fares and travel deals.
- Check an airline's safety and on-time records.
- View seating charts and choose your seat.
- Learn your travel rights.
- Develop a Plan B (alternative) in case Plan A fails.

If you've never compared flight options and pricing you are in for a surprise. There are many different fare basis, restrictions, and contingencies. You can check the same flight three times during the day and get totally different fare quotes. It's mind-boggling, but definitely enlightening.

Travel Wisdom: Airline fares and flight scheduling options vary dramatically. If you don't do your homework you will make unnecessary flight connections, fly at ungodly hours, and pay three times more than the guy sitting next to you.

Begin your homework by finding out what airlines serve your area or an airport within reasonable driving distance. Do this via the Internet, by calling the airport, or contacting a travel agent.

You'll quickly discover that all airlines are not created equal! There are major airlines, budget airlines and commuter airlines. Your choices are limited if you live in a small town served by only one carrier. Your choices are wide open if you fly out of a large metropolitan area, especially an airline "hub" such as Atlanta or Dallas.

Once you know what airlines are available to you, visit their websites. Learn all you can about that airline. Enter different travel dates and times and compare fares. Print the results for comparison. Often, airline websites offer special

Internet pricing and perks such as bonus frequent flyer mileage
for online booking. But wait! Don't click and purchase yet!
Explore all your options.

Look at major travel booking websites such as Orbitz,
Travelocity and Expedia. Orbitz is the travel website for
the big five major airlines: Delta, Continental, American,
Northwest, and United. It's a good site to check prices on
these carriers. Some low-fare airlines refuse to participate
in the site so you may miss other attractive alternatives.
Expedia allows you to research any airline, hotel and rental
cars. If the flight schedule you enter is not the cheapest one,
you will be offered alternatives for less. Travelocity is one
of the easiest sites to use. It also has a special "fare watcher"
feature that notifies you of fare sales relevant to your market.
Experiment with different travel dates and times for more
price comparisons on a variety of travel websites. Be sure to
note restrictions. Compare these results to those you found on
the airline websites.

> **Travel Wisdom: Develop a Plan B during your
> research. Expedia shows flights for all airlines serving
> your destination. Print all the flights listed and take it
> with you when you travel. If your original flight is
> delayed or cancels, you'll have some idea of the other
> options.**

You may have heard about airfare auction sites . . . where
you "name your own price." Check them out, but buyer
beware. They may be a viable source for last-minute travel
options, but there are significant drawbacks if you place a bid.
You have little or no control over when, how, or with whom
you fly. Your ticket is non-changeable and non-refundable. If
you don't know pricing, you may bid more than a ticket costs
with the airline or a travel agent. Once you place your bid and
it is accepted, you are stuck. If you make a mistake entering

your flight information you may find yourself with a ticket to
Athens, Greece rather than Athens, Georgia. When you place
a bid online and it is accepted, you have purchased the ticket.
Bidding is buying.

Significant Flight Factors to Consider:

- **Don't cut your travel day too close.** Leave a day early
  and include an overnight stay the day before the event,
  if you are traveling for a special celebration, critical
  business meeting, or to catch a cruise ship for a once-in-a-
  lifetime cruise. As a flight attendant, I saw many distraught
  travelers miss important events due to flight delays and
  cancellations.
- **Look for flights that leave early** If your flight cancels
  or is delayed, and you miss a connection, you have a full
  day to get back on track. Avoid the last flight of the day if
  possible. If you miss it, you are stuck overnight . . . often at
  your own expense.
- **Stay with the same airline**. Avoid connecting flights that
  change airlines unless there is no other choice. Changing
  airlines adds stress and increases the possibilities of
  problems.
- **Book a non-stop flight if you can.** Often airline
  reservations will tell you a flight is a *direct* flight. Sounds
  like you will go directly to your destination, right? Wrong.
  A direct flight makes one or more stops. True, you don't
  have to change airplanes and can usually stay onboard
  during stops. But, the more stops you make, the longer it
  takes to get there and the more chances for a delay. Also,
  watch out for flights with a *stopover.* This sounds like the
  flight makes a brief stop. A stopover flight is a connection
  that leaves you somewhere more than twenty-four hours.
  Unless the *stopover* is in a city with sights you've always
  wanted to see, look for another flight choice.

- **Avoid close connections unless you like to get your exercise dashing frantically through airports.** Making a flight connection is as simple as walking across the hall or to the gate next door or as complicated as waiting for a shuttle or train to another concourse or another terminal. Then, you still have a long, long hike to your connecting flight gate. Close connections cause problems! It's better to wait an hour or so than to misconnect by minutes and be stuck for several hours. Close connections also increase the possibility that even if you make the flight, your checked baggage won't.
- **Seat choices make a big difference in flight enjoyment or flight misery.** Sitting in a middle seat on a short flight is not a deal-breaker. Being stuck in a middle seat on a full flight for five hours coast-to-coast or transatlantic flight for eight hours is a miserable experience.

Travel Experience: One of our worse flight experiences almost ruined the memory of a perfect cruise. We used the cruise-provided air for the trip (something we rarely do). Big Mistake! We learned too late that we were booked on a World Airways charter from Barcelona to New York with a connection to Atlanta and another connection to Florida. We spent eight miserable hours in the most cramped middle seats imaginable. We missed our New York connection. We learned our lesson the hard way. Since that time, most cruise lines have started offering air deviations, allowing passengers to choose their airline and departure city for a minimal additional fee. Worth the cost! If deviation is not available, we book our own air travel instead of placing ourselves at the mercy of an outside booking source. We arrive a day early and pay for ship transfers.

After you've completed your homework, book your flight by calling airlines reservations, booking online, or call your travel agent. Don't know a travel agent? Check out the Yellow Pages and the chamber of commerce or ask around for recommendations. An experienced, well-connected travel agent can often find the best ticket price and facilitate other aspects of your trip. Don't be surprised to find that there is a fee for this service. Since airlines no longer pay commissions to travel agents, most of them charge a fee ranging from $10.00 to $25.00 per ticket. This fee is worth the few dollars for the experience and expertise a professional travel agent offers.

Travel Wisdom: If you book your flight online, get a printed confirmation. Follow-up with a call to airlines reservation to confirm your booking. The Internet is wonderful, but sometimes information disappears and the reservation you *think* is confirmed does not exist in airline records. Pay for all flight or other travel bookings with a major credit card. Credit card companies offer consumer protection when you do not get what you paid for.

Pros and Cons of Airline Seat Selection

When you make your reservation, it's time to select seats. Don't let a reservations agent decide where you sit. Look up seat selection charts on the airline's website. Be specific with your seat selection request when talking to a reservation agent or travel agent. Do not depend on "potluck seating."

A couple traveling together usually wants two-abreast seating. If two-abreast seating is not available, opt for adjacent aisle seats for maximum comfort and ease in deplaning. Three-abreast seats are good for a family of three, but no adult should have to endure the dreaded middle seat. A family of four will find two-and-two seating more comfortable than three-and-one. Airlines allow children under two years old to be held rather than having to purchase a seat. Think long and hard before you do this to save airfare. Children cannot be fastened into the same seat belt with an adult. In the event of severe turbulence or an emergency landing, it is impossible to hold an infant or small child. The safest and most comfortable way to travel with an infant or toddler is using an approved car seat in a passenger seat.

Location Matters

Seats Close To the Front:
Pros: Get off quickly on arrival.
(Important with quick connections.)
Cabin service usually begins in front.
(If there is any service.)
Seats in front are quieter because engines are over-wing or in the rear.
Cons: Boarding begins from the rear. Unless you have elite status and can board early, overhead bins may be filled and you will have to check your carry-on bag.

Seats in the Rear of the Aircraft
Pros: Board the aircraft first and have plenty of overhead space.
Cons: It takes forever to get off on arrival.
Since lavatories are in the rear, there is more aisle traffic, more noise & sometimes unpleasant odors.
More engine noise.
Seats in the last row do not recline and usually have no window.

Seats in the Over-Wing Area
Pros: Over-wing seats offer the smoothest ride.
There should still be sufficient overhead space.
If you are lucky and get an over-wing exit row, you'll have more leg room.
Disembarking won't take forever.
Cons: Avoid rows in front of over-wing emergency rows.
They don't recline.
The wing blocks your view of the ground.
Noise from wing-mounted engines and flaps.

Recommendation: Select seats in the over-wing area.

Travel Wisdom: Can't get the seats you want or unhappy with what you have? Try calling reservations after midnight; that's when reservations being held expire and more seats become available.

After booking your flight, there are still many factors that reduce air travel hassles and improve your flight experience.

Pack Less

Airlines have specific baggage guidelines and limitations. Limitations restrict size and weight of checked baggage and the size and number of carry-on bags. New security restrictions clearly list acceptable and unacceptable travel items. The less you take, the easier you clear security. On most domestic flights, you are allowed to check two pieces of luggage. Each checked bag cannot weigh more than 50 pounds. Overweight bags incur hefty fees. On international carriers, checked baggage weight is only 44 pounds per item. It can cost several hundred dollars if you exceed weight limits.

> **Travel Wisdom: Weigh your empty luggage. Older, hard-sided bags add critical pounds to your weight limits. The more your empty suitcase weighs, the less you can pack. Choose lightweight luggage and weigh your baggage at home while you can still adjust your travel needs.**

While packing, think ahead about travel attire and "small comforts" that make your flight more enjoyable. Dress for comfort on your flight. Wear loose-fitting knits that don't bind or wrinkle. Avoid pantyhose.

Top Ten Small Comforts for Air Travel

1. A small pillow for your back. Bring one or grab one on boarding before they disappear.
2. An inflatable neck pillow and lightweight blanket or wrap. Airlines do not clean pillows and blankets after each flight!
3. Tasty gourmet snacks.
4. Ear plugs and eye mask for undisturbed sleep on long flights.
5. Support socks to prevent legs and feet from swelling.
6. A great novel, magazines or crosswords.
7. Personal CD player and favorite music.
8. Toothbrush and other travel-size toiletries to freshen up.
9. Aromatherapy facial mist and eye drops to keep eyes moist and combat dry cabin air.
10. A bottle of water. Cabin service may be delayed or non-existent on some flights.

Think Carry-On

On short trips (one week or less), avoid checking baggage. The maximum size for carry-on bags is 45 linear inches. Those linear inches equate to a standard roller carry-on bag that is 20" long, 16" wide, and 9" deep. You can fit a lot of clothes in a bag that size if you choose the right travel wear and travel necessities. In addition to your carry-on bag, you are allowed one small personal item, such as a small briefcase or handbag

> **Travel Wisdom: For businesswomen. You are allowed one carry-on bag and one personal item. Cram a small handbag in your briefcase to avoid being singled out for having excessive carry-ons.**

If you check baggage, always keep a carry-on bag with you for "must have" items. Include at least one change of clothes in case your checked luggage does not arrive with you.

> **Travel Wisdom: Never pass up the chance for an earlier flight. Your original flight could be delayed or cancelled. *Plan ahead!* If you arrive at a connecting airport and find an earlier flight, guess what . . . you have to stay on the same flight as your checked baggage. And yes . . . the airlines do have a computer record of how many bags you checked and to where, so you can't fake it. And no . . . the airlines will not get your bags off the original flight to accommodate you. Carry-on bag only? Breeze right on that earlier flight and give yourself a pat on the back!**

> **More Travel Wisdom: Consider shipping most of your travel items for an extended stay at one location. The cost of shipping is far less than overweight fees. Shipping gifts, business presentations, samples and sports equipment saves valuable travel space and facilitates security clearance.**

Checked Baggage Smarts

All bags, checked and carry-on, are subjected to x-ray security. Plan accordingly to reduce the odds of being singled out for additional scrutiny.

- **Don't seal bags or clothing in plastic such as widely advertised vacuum-sealing clothing bags.** If your bags must be physically searched, your "de-vacuum packed" clothes will expand and may not fit back into the previous space they occupied.

- **Don't lock your bags.** If a checked bag must be opened for security reasons and you cannot be located to unlock the bag, it will not be boarded. Use plastic tie wraps instead of a keyed or combination lock. They are easily removed by security and security will usually replace them after the bag is searched. We also use baggage straps that wrap around the bag through the handle. They help prevent zipper failure, help identify our bags from the crowd, deter pilferage, but are easily removed by security if necessary.

- **Place identification on the outside and inside of all bags, checked and carry-on.** Use a business address rather than a home address to deter would-be thieves from scanning baggage addresses for home burglary opportunities. Include a copy of your travel itinerary and hotel address or cruise ship name and itinerary on the inside of your checked bag. If your baggage is lost, knowing where you are staying will speed up a reunion! This is a good time to put identification on other travel items, such as eyeglasses, cameras, laptops, and cell phones. Hundreds of personal items are left in airports and on airlines with no identification and little chance of being returned to the owners.

Travel Homework: Ever wonder what eventually happens to items left on airplanes? Take a look at www.unclaimedbaggage.com and find out.

- **Stand out from the crowd.** Mark your checked bags with colorful ribbons, colored electrical tape, stickers or other unique visible identifying marks. Reduce the chance someone will snatch your bag off the baggage carousel without bothering to check the identification tag.
- **Remove all old baggage destination tags before your checked baggage leaves your hands.**
- **Watch carefully as the ticket agent tags your checked bag. If you are making connections, be sure your bag is checked to your final destination.** Bags are tagged with a three-letter airport code. Know your destination code or ask. If you are traveling to DFW (Dallas) you don't want your bags to end up in DTW (Detroit). City codes are similar, the cities are not.
- **What to do when things go wrong?** (See *Chapter Seventeen—When Things Go Wrong.*)

Flight Departure Day

It's finally flight time. Before leaving home, double check your identification. Don't arrive at the airport without government-issued photo identification. If you don't have a driver's license or passport, military or government ID, contact your Drivers License Bureau and ask about a state-issued photo identification card. Be sure the name on your identification card and your ticket are exactly the same. On a honeymoon trip or after a recent divorce name change, take a copy of your marriage license or divorce decree to validate the name difference.

Cutting it close, arriving at the airport with minutes to spare before departure is a thing of the past. Here we go again: **PLAN AHEAD!** Allow plenty of time for traffic jams, airport parking, long check-in lines and longer security lines. At small airports with fewer flights, where you simply park close by and walk inside, arrive sixty to ninety minutes before scheduled departure. At a large metropolitan airport with multiple airlines and simultaneous flights and a remote parking lot with a shuttle bus to the terminal, allow two hours. On international flights, always arrive at the airport two and a half to three hours early. Hate the thought of sitting around the departure gate? You'll hate the stress of missing your flight more!

Travel Homework: If you don't travel often, do a "trial run" about a week before your flight. Visit the airport at the same day of the week and time of day you will be traveling. Check out parking logistics and cost. (You may find being dropped off by a friend or taxi is a better option than leaving your car in airport parking.) Note how long check-in and security lines are. Are food concessions open? Your "field trip" gives you a good idea of how much time you need. Allow extra time if weather is a factor on departure day.

If you cut it close and arrive at the gate minutes before departure, don't breathe a sigh of relief. Your seat may have been re-assigned. You will have to take whatever seats available—or be denied boarding. Don't add unnecessary stress to your travel day. Arrive early and people watch.

Travel Wisdom: Bypass long check-in lines by using the electronic check-in kiosks at major airports. Kiosk check-in is quick and simple. You need a frequent flyer number or the credit card you used to purchase your ticket. The kiosk "reads" your card and instructs you how to confirm your flight number and seat selection. You can change your seat selection if other seats are available. (Some kiosks allow self-baggage check-in, others do not. Another good reason for carry-on travel!) Once your seat selection is confirmed, the kiosk will issue your boarding pass and you are on your way. When you use the kiosk one time, you'll be hooked!

Taking the Stress Out Of Security

Clearing security may be simple and easy or complicated and stressful. While there are no guarantees you can breeze right through, there are steps to facilitate the process.

- **Know the current rules and comply with them without jokes or complaints.**
- **Check your bags carefully. Avoid inadvertently packing restricted items.** See Favorite Resources for websites with most current information.
- **Dress for success.** Avoid clothing and accessories that trigger sensitive metal detectors. Common items that "set off" detectors include: belt buckles, jewelry, metal buttons, watches, pocket change and underwire bras. High-heels, boots and most rubber-soled sneakers usually require removal. (It's easier just to take off heels/sneakers or boots toss them in a bin for x-ray and walk through the scanner in bare feet than to wear them, set off the alarm and be pulled aside for further body search.)

- **Love your jewelry?** I do! Eliminate security problems by placing jewelry in a Ziploc bag in your carry-on or handbag. Put it on after clearing security.
- **If you are delayed walking through the scanner, keep an eye on items placed on the conveyor belt for x-ray.** Although security is alert for theft, it is relatively easy for someone to scoop up your bag and leave the area. Place colorful ribbons or stickers on all baggage so that it stands out from the masses of black roller bags and is easy to keep in sight.
- **Prepare young travelers for security procedures**. They will take their cue from you. Explain what will happen and emphasize how important security is.
- **Pleasant cooperation is the order of the day.** Don't take it personally if you are singled out for further security checks. Comply without argument.

Welcome Aboard

Whew! You are finally on the airplane. Hopefully you've taken our repeated advice to "Plan Ahead" and you are ready to settle in for a pleasant flight. You have your "small comforts" and you'll be the envy of the other passengers as you indulge in your gourmet picnic you so wisely brought along.

Before you inflate your neck pillow, don your headsets and dive into your novel or settle down for a snooze, *stop, look and listen.* (Remember LACES.) Air travel is the safest way to travel. But, in the remote chance a problem does occur, how you react makes a life-or-death difference. Begin by testing your seat belt. Fasten and unfasten it several times. Be sure you can unfasten it without looking at it. If you're traveling with children, make a game of it. See who can fasten and unfasten their seat belt the quickest without looking at it.

Read the emergency card and pay attention to the flight

attendants' safety briefing. Locate your nearest exit and an alternate exit. Count the number of rows between your seat and the exit. In an emergency, visibility will be limited. If your flight is over water, feel under your seat for the life vest. Don't remove it . . . just be sure it's there. Stay awake and aware during take-off and landing.

In flight, keep your seat belt fastened at all times . . . not just when the Fasten Seat Belt sign is lit. Turbulence does not always announce itself. (See **Chapter Five— Travel Health and Safety** for additional in-flight safety tips.) Now, settle back and enjoy your flight!

Happy Landings

When the airplane begins the approach for landing, it's time to gather your belongings (especially the ones you stashed in the seat pocket in front of you). Put your shoes back on. Leave your carry-on bag under the seat until the aircraft reaches the terminal. Listen for in-flight announcements for connecting gates.

After landing, if you have plenty of time for your connection or are at your final destination, relax. Stay seated and let the masses stampede for the door. If your connection is close, every minute counts. Grab your carry-on bag and stampede with the rest. Avoid trampling old ladies and small children.

Pre-landing gate connection announcements are helpful, but don't trust them. Many passengers miss connections by dashing to a gate at the opposite end of the concourse or even another concourse only to find the "right" gate was right next door to their arriving flight. Gates often change and airplanes may switch flights. As you deplane, make a beeline for the nearest flight information monitor and double check your departing gate and departure time. If you need to grab a bite to eat or shop, be sure you arrive at your connecting gate thirty to forty-five minutes before departure.

At your final destination, proceed to baggage claim and hope for the best. Actually, statistics show that 97% of bags arrive on the correct flight. Encouragingly, only .005% of bags are permanently lost. The odds are on your side. Collect your bags. Check identification to be sure they are *your* bags and go your happy way.

No bag? Continue on to **Chapter Seventeen—When Things Go Wrong**!

Once you have tasted flight, you will forever walk the earth with eyes turned skyward, for there you have been, and there you will long to return.

— Leonardo da Vinci

CHAPTER FOURTEEN

RIDING THE RAILS

The journey is the reward. —— *Taoist saying*

Tired of the hassle of air travel? Want to see the scenery of the Rocky Mountains or quaint European villages without being in the driver's seat? If you enjoy leisurely travel, it's time to investigate travel by train. Riding the rails has attracted travelers for more than 170 years. With today's high-speed Acela trains, even business travelers are opting for taking the train in the New York-Boston-Washington corridor.

Advantages of Train Travel

- Travel from city center to city center avoiding airport hassles and traffic snarls.
- See some of the country's most breathtaking scenery.
- Relax in spacious 1st class seats at less than airline rates for coach seats.
- Rest in the comfort of a sleeper cabin instead of spending a miserable night in a cramped upright airline seat. (Reserve sleepers far in advance!)
- Socialize in the bar car and meet new friends.

- Enjoy a leisurely, freshly prepared meal in the dining car during meal hours or snacks from a food trolley.
- Take a stroll and stretch your legs without glares from flight attendants.

America by Train

Offering over five hundred destinations, Amtrak has routes all over the United States. You can research their schedules and fares on their website, **www.amtrak.com**. This website also offers special fare discounts. Always check for specials to your destination before making a reservation. Special fares may not be offered when you call the reservations number. For example, at the time *Travel Wisdom* was published, you could purchase a special fare National rail pass and ride Amtrak's entire system for thirty days for about $285.00— quite a savings over normal peak travel fare of $400.00 to $600.00. Another current option is a fifteen- to thirty-day pass for travel in certain regions such as the West for as little as $180.00. You can plan your itinerary to stop off and stay at various destinations along the way for as long as your pass lasts.

Popular Routes and Trains

Some of Amtrak's most popular routes provide the opportunity to see some of the most scenic parts of America, with the train serving as your mobile hotel. For instance:

The California Zephyr links Chicago to the West. This is one of the most scenic train rides in the country as you travel through the Rocky Mountains.

The Coast Starlight connects Seattle and Los Angeles. This is a scenic coastal route. Be sure to book travel time so you can enjoy the vistas during daylight hours. Book accommodations on the side of the train with the best views.

The Ethan Allen Express (nothing to do with the furniture store) winds from New York into Vermont. Book it during the fall season and marvel at the beautiful foliage.

The Adirondack travels between New York and Montreal and offers similar foliage vistas.

The Southwest Chief takes passengers through the landscapes of New Mexico and Arizona. You can almost imagine cowboys and Indians riding along with you.

The Crescent crosses twelve states all the way from New Orleans to New York. Lots of stops, but a great way to see the country if you are not in a hurry.

The Auto Train connects Washington, D.C. and Orlando. Your vehicle travels in an enclosed automobile/motorcycle car at the rear of the train, while you ride in comfort in a passenger car.

Two other popular trains, operating independently of Amtrak, are the **American Orient Express** and the **Alaska Railroad.** The American Orient Express operates out of cities like Washington DC, Los Angeles, New Orleans and Seattle. The atmosphere is one of days-gone-by elegance. Formally dressed attendants and train interiors with dark mahogany combined with gourmet dining and live entertainment make this train with its special itineraries a vacation dream. Similarly, the **Alaska Railroad** allows you to book customized travel packages out of Anchorage, Seward or Fairbanks.

Train Accommodation Choices

In the United States, your choices are basically coach and private sleeper compartments. If you're taking a short trip where the primary focus is to get from Point A to Point B, coach service is the most economical choice. Coach cars offer reclining seats with fold-down tables and room for carry-on bags overhead. Unlike cramped airline seats, there is plenty of leg room and wide windows to allow you to watch the passing scenery. Dining cars or snack bars offer quick sandwiches and snacks or gourmet meals and bar service. Cost of meals is not included with coach fare tickets.

On longer trips, whether overnight or cross country, sleeper compartments allow you to relax in privacy during the day in reclining seats that make into berths at night. Some sleepers have private toilets and sinks; others have community restrooms and showers nearby. Your attendant makes up your bed at night and supplies you with clean towels. In the morning, he/she will wake you with coffee. Sleepers range from one- and two-person standards to deluxe sleepers with private sink, shower, toilet and vanity, to family-size compartments. Well worth the cost on long trips! Meals are complimentary with sleeper bookings. Special handicapped-accessible sleepers are available with food and beverage service to the room.

On-Board Atmosphere

On most trains, the atmosphere is relaxed and friendly. Passengers tend to mix and mingle, unlike airline passengers who are herded on and off with few pleasantries. It is easy to walk around and visit other cars, including a domed sightseeing car, dining car and lounge car. There is time for a game of cards with family or newfound acquaintances. Time to read a good book . . . or simply revel in the scenery constantly unfolding outside large picture windows. Be sure to take a map to track where you are and what scenery is coming up.

Amtrak offers expanded menus on all long-distance trains. A full-service dining car serves three hot meals a day, including seafood specialty dishes and decadent chocolate mousse cake! Be sure to check whether or not dining reservations are required on your trip.

> **Travel Experience: One of our favorite short train travel experiences was a trip aboard the Napa Valley Wine Train. This three-hour, thirty-six-mile trip begins in Napa and winds through Napa Valley vineyards to St. Helena and returns to Napa. We enjoyed a delicious champagne brunch and met interesting fellow travelers.**

Rail Travel in Europe

Train travel is one of the best ways to see Europe. If you fly into almost any European city, there are direct links to train terminals. In fact, train stations are located inside many airports in cities such as Amsterdam, Barcelona, Berlin, Brussels, London, Paris, Rome and Zurich (just to name a few). Leaving the airport, Europe's rail system stretches over one hundred thousand miles and takes you through cities, quaint villages and breathtaking scenery.

There are several choices of accommodations on board. There are First Class seats, Second Class seats, sleepers and couchette accommodations. Second Class seats are the least expensive with more seats per car. First Class seats are much more spacious and recline. Sleeper accommodations vary from single and double compartments to a "dormitory" type (couchette) arrangement that accommodates six passengers (both male and female mixed) in closely spaced bunks with no other amenities. Note: Couchettes are usually found only in Second Class.

If you are only traveling by train from one city or country to another (point to point), we recommend First Class seats. Traveling long distances or overnight, you will find a sleeper more private and comfortable.

> **Travel Wisdom: Reservations are required for sleeper cabins. Make your reservation at least sixty days or more in advance to avoid disappointment.**

European Train Ticketing

Fare options are practically endless. Point-to-point tickets are available for a single trip from one destination in Europe to another destination. Again, unless you are on a tight budget, choose the nominally more expensive First Class fare.

If you plan to travel extensively throughout Europe, your best bet will be a Railpass or Eurailpass. A Railpass allows unlimited travel for a specific number of days within one country or region. The Eurailpass offers more flexibility with two categories of travel options. Eurailpasses provide unlimited First Class travel throughout seventeen countries. Eurailpasses can be purchased for fifteen, twenty-one, thirty, sixty, and ninety days. There are also other Eurailpass options for group, senior and youth travel.

> **Travel Wisdom: Buying a ticket allows you to board the train, but does *not* guarantee you a seat on most trains in Europe. An additional reservation fee is necessary to have a guaranteed seat of your choice. Tickets can be purchased 120 days in advance.**

Premier Trains

Don't miss the opportunity to travel on one of Europe's high-speed Premier Trains, with intriguing names such as *Alaris, Artesia, Cisalpino, Thalys* and *Eurostar*. These ultra-modern trains are loaded with extra features to make your trip special. Most First Class Premier Train tickets include a meal served at your seat, newspapers, welcome aboard drinks, and other amenities. Over a dozen countries offer Premier Train service.

The *Eurostar* is the most famous of the Premier Trains. It travels from London to Paris in about three hours and runs on an hourly basis. Also called the Channel Tunnel Train, The Eurostar crosses through the channel tunnel between Great Britain and continental Europe in only twenty minutes. It is the epitome of service, comfort and a unique travel adventure. Another advantage to travel on the *Eurostar* is that your seat reservation is included in the price of your ticket. No additional fee is required.

On *Eurostar*, there are three types of seating available: First Premium Class, First Class, and Standard Class. Standard Class includes your seat reservation and food cart service. No other amenities. First Class reservations include a seat reservation, a newspaper, a complimentary drink and meal served at your seat. First Premium Class includes the same amenities as First Class and offers a greater selection of food and drinks and a complimentary taxi transfer in Paris or London.

Ten Tips to Improve Travel by Train

1. **Shop around before you purchase a ticket or pass in the U.S. or Europe.** Promotions are common and new bargains appear on short notice.
2. **Read the fine print. In fact, examine your ticket jacket carefully.** Be sure you understand the terms and conditions.
3. **Guard rail passes carefully.** They are *not* replaceable if lost or stolen.
4. **Always have a Plan B.** Although not as frequent as in air travel, cancellations and delays do occur. Pick up a timetable and map out alternatives in case of unexpected

changes. Use a cell phone or calling card to expedite changes.

5. **Double and triple check where your train leaves from and goes to.** Some cities have more than one train station (Paris has six). Confirm your itinerary with the information booth at the station. If there is a language problem, write down the name of the city you are traveling to and departure time. The information clerk will usually nod agreement.

6. **Be sure you are in the "right" car. Never assume the whole train is going where you are.** Sometimes cars are dropped off along the way. Be sure your car has your destination displayed on the nameplate as you board.

7. **Travel light. Pack smart.** Not much different than any other travel. See *Chapter Two—Packing Smart.* Be certain you can handle your luggage. Porters are not always available.

8. **Practice good personal security.** Don't leave baggage unattended. Keep your valuables concealed with money belts. Use a bicycle lock to secure your baggage to your seat or overhead rack while you sleep. Locate exits and use the **LACES** principles.

9. **Study your route and plan ahead to enjoy the best scenery.** Ask which side of the train will have the best views. Use a map to follow your route and know what is coming ahead.

10. **Relax and enjoy the ride.** Talk to other travelers and make new friends.

Check out the *Resources* section of **Travel Wisdom** for additional information sources on traveling by rail.

CHAPTER FIFTEEN

HIGHWAYS AND BY-WAYS

For many travelers, a driving vacation is the best way to visit a destination. They prefer to drive the family car, or rent a car or recreational vehicle. If you are on a tight budget, you can still enjoy a vacation. At long-distance fly-in destinations, many travelers rent a car to have more freedom to explore the area.

If you decide to fly to a destination and rent a car on arrival, compare costs with airline "Fly-and-Drive" programs. You won't find this option through airline reservations. Call the airline's vacation package department. You can find the telephone number for vacation travel on the airline website or call reservations and ask for it. When you call the vacation department, tell the agent you are interested in a quote on a Fly-and-Drive package

In major cities, don't be surprised if the total package price is less than airline fare booked on Internet or reservations. For example, I priced a roundtrip airfare for two people to San Francisco staying four days. The fare was $665.00 per person. A rental car for four days added another $125.00. Total trip for two added up to $1455.00. A call to the vacation division resulted in a Fly and Drive package that included airfare and an intermediate-size vehicle for a total price of $998.00 for two. A significant saving. This approach is not always the most economical, but it's certainly worth a call to compare.

RV travel, up over 20% in the past two years, is a popular option for would-be travelers who want to avoid air travel. With over sixteen thousand RV parks across the United States, whether you want the seashore, the mountains, or anywhere in-between, there is a parking place with your name on it. Many parks or campgrounds offer amenities such as beachfront locations, swimming pools, game rooms, golf, and cook-out facilities. More and more RVs are seen cruising down the highway bearing the bumper sticker, "Roughing It Smoothly."

Advantages of a Driving Vacation

- No airport hassles.
- Easy to take the kids and pets.
- Bring more . . . fewer packing problems.
- Travel on your own schedule.
- Costs less than air travel.
- Enjoy the scenery along the way.
- Easier to control accommodation and food budget.
- Enjoy leisurely conversation, road games, and books on tape.

Advantages of RV Travel

In addition to the above benefits of highway travel, RV enthusiasts add these perks:
- Take everything you need to have fun: sports/beach equipment, books, videos, games, family photos, your favorite pillow—the list is endless. The RV is your home away from home.

- No need to constantly pack and unpack. Everyone can have their "things" organized and handy.
- Enjoy all the comforts of home and sometimes more. Today's RV is equipped with everything from air-conditioning to satellite dishes . . . from A to Z.
- Have meals and snacks right from your own kitchen . . . whenever you wish. No need to rely on fast food stops for a snack and the restroom.
- Usually less expensive than staying in a hotel, especially during peak travel times.
- Good way to visit family without being underfoot.
- Enjoy the camaraderie of parks and campgrounds. Meet new friends.

There are also some driving drawbacks to consider. Traffic jams, road hazards, breakdowns, and careless drivers create stress for the driver and passengers . . . and take a toll on tempers by the end of some days. Bickering, boredom and blabbering can strain any family's togetherness.

As with all types of travel, careful planning, flexibility and a sense of humor help alleviate problems.

Planning Ahead for a Road Trip

1. **Schedule a complete maintenance check-up well before your trip**. Change oil and other fluids. Inspect and change filters, wiper blades, hoses and belts. Have tires checked for wear and tire pressure. Don't forget the spare tire!
2. **Put together a road safety kit.** Make sure you have a fire extinguisher, emergency bottles of water, emergency tire inflation canister, road flares, a basic automotive tool kit, and first aid kit. In winter, add a warm blanket. Take along at least one spare car key.
3. **Invest in AAA or another roadside assistance program.** Hopefully, it's insurance you won't need, but can be a life

and sanity saver. Most companies offer additional cost-saving benefits in addition to standard roadside protection.

4. **Be sure your driver's license and insurance are current.** Place proof of insurance, registration and roadside assistance information in a folder in the glove compartment or console.

5. **Never travel without a cell phone** for emergencies, to keep in touch with family back home, or to notify hotels/guides of arrival time changes.

6. **Collect maps and driving directions. (See Travel Resources for some good Internet mapping websites.)** Choose a compact map and mark landmarks, attractions, and rest stops for older children to follow along. Give simple lessons in map-reading, including mileage calculations, and make a game of "how much farther is it?"

7. **Traveling with children.** Be sure to pack favorite toys, no-mess snacks, no-spill beverages, and security blankets. Plan a few surprise snacks and gifts along the way to keep everyone on their toes. Wet wipes and a towel come in handy. A lap desk for drawing or eating is convenient. Schedule regular rest and fun stops for working off pent-up energy. Play family travel games with prizes.

8. **Traveling with a pet.** Check with the vet a week or two before you leave. Be sure shots are up to date and ask about medication to make travel easier. Take current vaccination records. Just as you do with children, bring your pet's regular food, favorite snacks and toys. Don't forget drinking water and a plastic bowl. Be sure collar has ID information and keep a photo of your pet with other travel documents. Are your planned accommodations pet-friendly? At rest stops, keep your pet on a leash and use a "pooper-scooper."

9. **Plan your drive time.** Traveling through scenic territory, plan daytime driving so you won't miss the sights. Traveling with young children, night or very early morning departures may encourage sleep and maintain peace and quiet for hours

on end. Don't over-schedule. Recognize when you hit your limit and need to recharge your personal battery.

10. **Load your car inside the garage so that by-passers don't know you are leaving.** Notify trusted neighbors or the local police that you will be away and if anyone is expected to stay at or check on your home.

Highway Entertainment

Here are four of our favorite family games to pass the hours on the road:

- **Counting Four-Legged Animals.** Each person picks one side on the road and counts all four-legged animals for a set period of time. If you pass a cemetery, all animals must be buried and you must start over. Pass a pond or lake, your animals drown and you must start over. Give a prize or reward for the most animals during a set period of time. (Obviously, this game works best in a rural setting.)

- **The Alphabet Game.** Each traveler picks one side of the road and beginning with the letter "A" finds each letter of the alphabet in order at the beginning of a word on roadside signs. First player to reach "Z" wins the prize/reward. (Hank and I occasionally find ourselves still playing this game when we travel by car along boring stretches of interstate highways with a lot of advertising billboards.)

- **Car Bingo.** Long ago we bought a set of sturdy bingo cards with photos of things along the roadside. Sliding windows covered object once spotted. Winner is first player to cover all windows on the card. The website **www.momsminivan.com** has printable car bingo games and other great resources.

- **Books on Tape.** Books on tape have entertained us for many hours on the road. It is also worthwhile to rent a video player and bring along a stack of children's movies and cartoons.

Travel Experience: When our sons were very young, we frequently traveled by car to visit family and on vacations. One of our tactics to help eliminate whining and constant questions of "how much longer is it" was to give each boy a roll of quarters at the beginning of the trip. Each time there was whining, tattletales or the how-much-longer question, the offender had to give up one of his quarters. Our older son always arrived at our destination with all of his quarters intact. Our younger son would begin throwing quarters from the backseat to the front the last hour or so, having decided that good behavior was not worth the price.

Car and RV Rentals

Maybe you don't want to put the wear and tear on your personal automobile. Maybe you are flying to a destination and need a car after arrival. Maybe you don't want the expense of owning an RV, but would like to try RV'ing on your next vacation. Fortunately, renting a car or an RV in the United States is simple and cost effective.

Research rental vehicles as you do airlines, hotels, or tours. Begin with the Internet, yellow pages, or your travel agent. Internet research is a particularly good way to compare rates and terms. All of the major suppliers have good websites that allow you to shop around for dates, vehicle models, and options. Many websites offer Internet specials.

Consider these guidelines for researching and renting a vehicle for business or pleasure travel:

- **Plan ahead.** (Where have you heard that before?)
- **Compare before you commit.** No single company always has the best rates. You can compare by calling individual major companies and asking for their best rate/deal. You

can save time by running an online comparison with a website like www.travelocity.com. Enter your travel destination and dates and compare rates, makes of cars, insurance terms, and specials. Print comparisons and review for your personal best deal. (Don't forget to also compare prices with airline Fly and Drive divisions)

- **Join car rental clubs before you make your reservation.** A few firms charge a membership, most don't. Even if you rent infrequently, club membership can save you time and money and improve customer service. Most clubs can be joined online at the agency website.

- **If you are keeping the vehicle four or five days, compare the weekly rental with the daily rental.** Often the weekly rate will be better and you can simply turn the car in early.

- **Take the most economical car that meets your needs.** That said, don't make the mistake of taking the smallest car especially for more than two adults. If you are keeping the vehicle several days and plan on covering a lot of territory, it will get smaller by the mile. Compare rates for an intermediate size or better. Saving a few dollars is not worth the discomfort of being cramped in a compact car for hours on end. Convenience options such as cruise control and a cassette/CD player are also worth the few extra dollars for long hours on the road

- **Watch out for add-on charges.** Most initial rates quoted are basic rates and do not include a variety of additional fees. (1) Local or airport taxes can add 10% or more to your daily rental. (2) Insurance can easily add $20.00 per day or more. Check your personal automobile insurance coverage. It may cover you for rentals at no extra charge. Some major credit cards also offer no-cost collision coverage when you use their card. Even homeowners policies cover some aspects of theft of personal items from the car. Point here, don't pay for duplicate coverage. (3) Watch for extra driver charges. The access fee for additional drivers is often $5.00

per day or more. (4) Fuel surcharges can add unnecessary dollars to your total rental. If you don't return the vehicle with a full fuel tank, you may pay an outrageous per-gallon fuel charge. (5) Charges for child safety seats may run an additional $2–$5 per day.

- **Keep your eye on the "24-hour clock."** If you pick your car up on Tuesday at 3 p.m. and return it before 3 p.m. on Wednesday, you will be charged for one day. Go over the 24-hour period and you may be charged for an entire extra day or at least a high hourly rate for the extra hours. Read the fine print and clarify.
- **Make sure you are getting what you think you are getting.** Most car companies offer unlimited mileage. Don't assume you have unlimited mileage.
- **Ask for a spare key.** Accidents happen. If you accidentally lock your key in the car or lose it, several hundred miles from the pick-up location, you have a problem . . . one that could get expensive.
- **Check and double check the car before you drive away.** Check for damage. Locate and learn how to operate the lights, wipers, air conditioner/heater, emergency brake, gas cap, trunk and hood releases, turn signals, cruise control, radio, lights and flashers. Be sure everything works properly.
- **Avoid substantial drop-off charges if possible.** Picking a car up in one city and dropping it off in another city may not cost extra...or may be as much as several hundred dollars. **Don't assume. Ask.**

Driving International Highways

If you are considering renting a car and driving outside the United States, research becomes even more important. Every country has its own laws. Car rental contracts and road signage may not be in English. You may have to drive on the "wrong" side of the road. Be sure you can handle the differences. Then, in some countries driving can be dangerous and very expensive and it's in your best interest to leave the driving to local transportation providers. Know before you go. A good source of information on international driving is **www.travelocity.com/city.com and www.fodors.com/ traveltips/carrental**.

If you decide to drive yourself, in most countries you will need an international driver's permit (IDP). This IDP translates your driver's license information into eleven languages and is recognized by 150 countries. The IDP doesn't replace your driver's license. You need both. There are only two agencies in the U.S. authorized to issue an IDP. They are the American Automobile Association (AAA) and the American Automobile Touring Alliance. For more information on obtaining an IDP, contact your local AAA office and complete an application. You must get the permit before leaving home and don't wait until the last minute. These cautions are intended to prepare you, not to totally discourage you from driving abroad.

We don't drive on most trips outside the United States. We prefer to be passengers enjoying the scenery and dialogue of an experienced driver and travel guide.

Continue on for an excerpt from our travel journal about our favorite driving vacation.

CHRISTEN'S TRAVEL JOURNAL
DRIVING THROUGH WINE COUNTRY

Day One. Our flight arrives on time and we find the rental car agency with no problem. Always a good start. Half an hour later, we are in the midst of San Francisco noon rush hour. (There seems to always be a rush hour here.) Hank is the driver and I am the navigator. Progress is slow, but we gradually work our way out of the city and head for Napa Valley and our first bed-and-breakfast reservation.

I've been researching this trip on the Internet for weeks. We've opted to stay at bed-and-breakfasts for the next eight days. All the accommodations we booked advertised incredible gourmet champagne breakfasts and afternoon wine and cheese hours. We look forward to meeting fellow travelers with a similar love for travel and vino!

After a couple of wrong turns, and a steep drive up a winding road to the top of a ridge, we arrive at the Bylund House in St. Helena, our home away from home for the next two nights. Right away, we realize this is really different from checking into the Holiday Inn. There is no one home. There is a huge dog lying on the front steps. We sit in the car a few minutes and decide to cautiously approach the house since we can see what appears to be a note taped to the front door. Thank goodness, the dog is friendly . . . or maybe just disinterested . . . definitely not a fierce guard dog. Although the note doesn't have our name on it, it welcomes "Dear Guests" and tells us to go around back to the "tower." Our room is at the top. We climb the stairs to the third floor and are greeted with a breathtaking view of rolling hills and the surrounding valley in three directions. Hank (being an ex-firefighter) hopes there are no brush fires during our stay. The view and the room are beautiful. There are wonderful amenities such as cozy bathrobes, orchids, truffles, and aromatherapy candles. We wander down to the living room area and are welcomed with another note telling us there is chilled wine and snacks in the refrigerator. There is a large selection of music and stacks of local guides and intriguing coffee books. We make ourselves at home. The thought does occur that since the note on the door did not have our name on it and nothing says Bylund House, we could be in the wrong place, eating someone else's food, and drinking their wine. Oh well, we'll see what happens.

Late afternoon, our hosts come home and we find we are the right guests at the right B & B. Bill and Diane Bylund are a delightful couple. Bill is an architect and has done design work on many local wineries. Diane is an attorney. They are a wealth of information. We enjoy cocktail hour with them before we head into St. Helena for dinner.

Day Two. After a delicious breakfast, we head out to visit the wineries we have chosen for the day. Bill suggests some additional stops. At home, 10 a.m. might be a bit early for popping a cork and sampling wine; here it seems the natural thing to do. There are two main arteries through Napa Valley, Highway 29 and the Silverado Trail. We decide to work our way down Highway 29 in the St Helena area. Although we have a couple of stops pre-planned, we stop at several wineries that have "curb-side" appeal. Some of these impulsive stops turn out to be our favorites. From our research, we know that tastings vary greatly from one winery to another. Some tasting rooms require reservations. Most wineries charge a nominal tasting fee, usually from $3.00 to $5.00 applied to purchase if you buy a bottle of wine.

We begin at the first winery built in Napa Valley after prohibition, Merryvale Vineyards. We move on to several other wineries, but discover quickly we have to pace ourselves. Three tastings seems to be the limit before a break.

A favorite stop today is V. Sattui Winery. Wines here are sold only at the winery. The grounds are beautifully landscaped. It's the perfect place for a picnic. We select our picnic items at the gourmet deli and cheese shop and seek out a shady spot to enjoy our feast. This is one of our *travel moments*.

After our morning tastings and lunch, we spend a little time browsing the shops of St. Helena and enjoy a shopping spree at Dean & Deluca. It's time for a few more afternoon tastings

and head back to Bylund House. Again, we enjoy sitting by
the lap pool, having late-afternoon wine with our hosts. After
dinner in town, we head back for an early night. We have an
early morning tomorrow with reservations for lunch on the
Napa Valley Wine Train.

The night is crystal clear, a little chill in the air. There seem
to be more stars twinkling in the sky outside our windows than
we've ever seen. We sleep with the curtains open and windows
raised to enjoy the fresh air and wake to a beautiful sunrise.

Day Three. After breakfast, we head into Napa for a trip
on The Wine Train. This railway adventure turns out to be
a highlight of our visit. We begin our three-hour journey in
the lounge car, enjoying champagne and light appetizers.
Fellow travelers are friendly, and interesting conversations
flow. Lunch in the dining car is a multi-course delight. We
savor each course as we watch the vineyards sliding past our
window.

Following our trip, we make a couple of stops on the
way "home" to Bylund House. This evening, we mention to
Bill that we love champagne. He suggests that we try to get
reservations to tour Shramsberg Champagne caves as we leave
Napa tomorrow.

Day Four. We call Shamsberg and are told there are
reservations available if we can be there by 9 a.m.; that's in
twenty minutes and we are fifteen minutes away. We toss our
bags in the car, say our good-byes, and hit the trail out of St.
Helena. The Shramsberg tour is an incredible experience. The
caves are fascinating. We learn so much about champagne and
even get a chance to see a riddler in action! The tasting, at
$12.00, is worth twice the cost. It takes place in the tasting
room of the caves at an elegantly set table with beautiful
crystal glasses. The grounds are equally impressive.

As we continue to the Sonoma region, we make several
other impulsive stops. At one of these stops, we ride the aerial
tram ride to the top of a ridge where Sterling Vineyards offers

a well-planned, self-guided tour through their winery. We enjoy the tasting by the cozy fireplace.

By late afternoon, we are in Healdsburg at the Grape Leaf Inn. What a wonderful B & B! The Grape Leaf Inn is as colorful as its name. It's a romantic old Victorian home with wraparound porches, skylights over the bed and a spa bathtub (for two) also under a skylight.

Our host, Richard Rosenberg, holds late-afternoon wine tastings, bringing in wine experts from local wineries for lively discussions. We notice several fellow travelers entering notes in wine journals along with labels from their favorite vineyard tours of the day. We learn that all the wineries have baskets of complimentary beautiful labels for their wines. Wow! Why didn't we think of that? Tomorrow we will buy a wine journal. Wish we had collected labels at our favorite wineries in Napa! One of the best parts of travel is what you learn along the way.

Day Five. We wander down to breakfast and are amazed at the spread before us. Grand Marnier Croissant French Toast and Fresh Asparagus and Parmesan Cheese Soufflé. Got to have the recipes. Richard graciously shares them. We head into Sonoma and enjoy another full day visiting local wineries and shopping. Our favorite tastings and tours here are Ravenswood, Gloria Ferrer Champagne Caves, and Ferrari-Carrano Vineyard and Winery. It is a beautifully manicured paradise. Wonderful wines. Great gift shop. Hank purchases a wooden wine box. How will we get it home? Easy, we put it in our suitcase and pack our clothes in the wine box. He already has plans to build a wine table around his find. Late afternoon, another wine lesson and tasting at the Grape Leaf Inn.

About midnight, we are awakened by a brief thunderstorm. It is worth waking to watch the lightning play across the sky and listen to a symphony of thunder and rain as we lie beneath the skylight. Another *travel moment.* It's worth waking to see a moment that takes your breath away!

After another superb breakfast of white chocolate pancakes and a variety of side dishes, we regretfully leave the Grape Leaf Inn and continue north toward Mendocino and the coast. As we drive through the towering redwoods, we stop frequently to savor the fresh pine scent and walk through the forests. At times the forest is so dense that there is little daylight and we have to drive with the headlights on. The road is winding and driving difficult. No wine tasting today, but what an experience. As we approach the coast, the scenery changes around each bend. We leave the dense forest and hug the coastline hundreds of feet above the Pacific Ocean.

Our reservations for the next two days is at the Little River Inn. We arrive late afternoon. Our reservation is for a cozy cabin across the highway from the ocean. We ask about the cottages on the coast side. They are the "honeymoon cottages." The hostess suggests we take a key and look at one to see if we want to upgrade. As we open the door, we are breathless. Sliding glass doors across the entire back of the cottage frame a view straight out into the Pacific Ocean. There is a large private deck with a hot tub. There's a king-sized bed in the combination living/bedroom and the fireplace is stacked with firewood for a cozy evening. We're sold!

After check-in, we enjoy a bottle of champagne and watch the sunset on our deck before crossing over to the Little River Inn for dinner.

At 5 a.m., Hank wakes me to share another *travel moment.* There is a full moon and the ocean is lit as bright as day. The bells on the buoys are ringing and we hear sea lions barking.

Day Seven. We have a full day to discover Mendocino. I decide in my next life, this is where I want to be. We climb down the steep slope and spend hours exploring the coves below the cliffs. We drive into Fort Bragg and load a shopping basket with huge dungeness crabs and other gourmet delights for a special dinner in front of a crackling fire back at the cottage. Another *travel moment.* This trip has been full of *travel moments.*

Day Eight. Time to head down the coast toward San Francisco. It is a harrowing drive, but worth every minute of it. Pretzel twists and turns with only narrow right of ways separate us from dropping hundreds of feet into the ocean. We take it slow . . . in spite of log trucks bearing down on our bumper. We stop mid-day in Bodega Bay, the location of the famous Hitchcock movie, *The Birds*. We enjoy another incredible seafood lunch. Got to go on a diet when we get home

Late afternoon finds us back in San Francisco for a couple of nights with friends before heading home. We enjoy dinner and share our adventures.

Ending Note: We're not usually driving travelers, but we would recommend this trip to anyone. We enjoyed it so much, we are planning a repeat in the near future. Next time we'll bring our Wine Journal.

CHAPTER SIXTEEN

VACATIONING AT HOME

The great opportunity is where you are. Every place is under the stars, every place is the center of the world.
— John Burroughs

No desire to "see the Pyramids along the Nile?" No budget for travel to faraway places? Don't despair. Don't overlook the benefits and pleasures of vacationing in or near your hometown.

Advantages of Travel Near Home

- No airline hassles.
- Easy to pack. Forget something? Zip home and pick it up.
- Take advantage of off-season prices, special offers, and last-minute trips.
- Supports local economy.
- Build a mini-vacation around a special interest. (i.e., cooking or golf.)
- Can usually cancel up to three days before with no penalty.
- Invite friends and family to "visit" your vacation.
- Take numerous mini-vacations at less cost than one faraway trip.

- Try new restaurants, hotels, attractions in your own backyard.
- Get local resident's discounts.
- Good way to practice solo travel.

> **Travel Experience: One of our favorite travel-at-home trips is an annual Valentines Day getaway. We take turns planning the weekend. (So what if Valentine's Day isn't on the weekend. Remember flexibility is a key travel trait.) A couple of years ago, Hank booked a wonderful Valentines Day package at the Ramada Inn Beach Resort . . . fifteen minutes from our house. Our getaway included a suite for one night, champagne and strawberries, a romantic dinner for two, and champagne brunch the next morning. We enjoyed a walk on the beach at sunset and a relaxing, romantic evening for the two of us. Total cost (due to off-season rates) was under $200.00. This year we ventured a little farther from home . . . thirty minutes away . . . and reserved a one-bedroom condo at Baytowne Wharf, Sandestin, Florida. The first evening, we had a gourmet picnic in our condo and a rose petal bath. A champagne breakfast the next morning, a cooking class at Gerard's Cajun Cookery at noon, and a late-afternoon massage at the spa capped off the next day. We were having so much fun, we decided to stay an extra night. We savored a dinner at Bistro Bijou, and spent the next morning relaxing and reading on our private patio before journeying the half hour home.**

Discovering Vacations At Home

Research vacations at home as you do vacations cross country or abroad. It's much easier to take advantage of last-minute offers and to change plans when necessary. Try these local research ideas:

- **Play tourist.** Visit your local Chamber of Commerce or Visitor's Center and load up on brochures for local accommodations, restaurants, and attractions. Ask about discount coupons and special offers. If you live in a rural area or small town with no local vacation opportunities, look close by. We consider hometown turf anywhere within a two- or three-hour drive.

- **Plan getaways around holidays such as a romantic Valentine, Birthday or Anniversary Getaway.** Make up your own holiday. Put together a Rest & Relaxation Weekend, a Girlfriend's Retreat, or a Just-For-Me sabbatical. Surprise your spouse or significant other with a Mystery Outing. Plan an overnight getaway. Pack your bags, but don't tell your guest where you are going until you arrive. Another idea. Plan your weekend or overnight and you check-in alone. Leave clues at home and have your spouse follow clues or a treasure map and discover where you are.

- **Plan a mini-vacation around a business trip or family event.** Tag along with your spouse or a friend when they are attending a business meeting or seminar and staying overnight. Enjoy a partially expense-paid treat. Host a family reunion or make a local family wedding a weekend affair.

> **Travel Experience: Hank's company sometimes sponsors local conferences. As a host, he must stay at the conference hotel. I "tag along" and enjoy the fringe benefits with only my meals as an expense and get bonus time together.**

Travel Experience: One year we hosted a family reunion in Ft. Walton Beach. By planning off-season, we were able to negotiate good rates for multiple rooms. We stayed at a resort with cookout facilities and enjoyed picnics on the beach with volleyball tournaments and sand castle building contests. Hank escorted the men on a guided tour of the Naval Air Museum in Pensacola (thirty-seven miles away) to the local Air Force Armament Museum. Lynne took the women shopping and arranged childcare for afternoon manicures and pedicures. Older teens and young adults rented a pontoon boat and enjoyed local water activities. We also chartered a sailboat for a beautiful sunset cruise. We renewed family ties and enjoyed stress-free host duties on our local "Family Vacation."

- **Stay alert for special interest events and activities in your area.** Check with the chamber of commerce or local newspaper for a yearly calendar of events. Watch newspapers for upcoming event press releases and advertisements.

Travel Experience: We are cooking and wine enthusiasts. So, when we spotted a press release for a weekend cooking school at the Sandestin Hilton (thirty minutes from home) we were quick to sign up. The weekend was presented by Cooking Pleasures. The cost for the weekend was $450.00 per couple. This charge included a beautiful gulf-front room for two nights, eight cooking classes, food demonstrations, and a wine tasting. Since we dined on dishes prepared by the guest chefs, our other expenses were minimal. We were surprised that there was only one other "local" there. We enjoyed playing the local experts to guests from all over the country.

- **Research websites for local accommodations, restaurants and attractions ideas.** That's where out-of-towners find their ideas and travel deals. Include research on auction sites such as EBay and Yahoo. It's easy to verify any offers you find in your own backyard.

> **Travel Wisdom: We frequently purchase gift certificates at half price for restaurants in our hometown at www.restaurants.com and on www.ebay.com. When we travel out of town, we check out restaurants at our destination and often purchase dining certificates for use there. Log on to www.restaurants.com and click on the state you are visiting from the drop-down box. Next click on the city within that state. We recently paid $5.00 for a 50% gift certificate for a party of six at a new hometown restaurant. We also paid half-price for two $25.00 gift certificates for restaurants in Charleston, South Carolina to use on a business trip.**

- **Bid on local getaway packages at charity auctions.** Weekend packages are popular silent and live auction bid items. You can contribute to a good cause . . . and enjoy the benefits.

Discover travel at home. We believe you'll be hooked. When you travel close to home, you will find it easy to relax, refresh, and rejuvenate and return . . . again and again.

CHAPTER SEVENTEEN

WHEN THINGS GO WRONG

Things don't go wrong, they simply happen.
— *Jacob Ghitis*

We've traveled extensively all over the world during the past twenty years, including fourteen cruises. Amazingly, our trips flowed without a hitch . . . other than very minor inconveniences. We hear travel horror stories from fellow travelers. We read news stories about trips "gone bad." We have friends and relatives who often seem to have unfortunate travel experiences. Are we just lucky? Sometimes "Murphy's Law" kicks in with a vengeance and best-laid plans go awry. Human nature also plays a strong role in travel travail. A minor inconvenience to one person . . . may be a disaster to someone else.

There is no guaranteed way to avoid travel problems. There are precautions to take to avoid some travel problems . . . and steps to minimize the consequences when problems do occur.

Some travel problems arise from misunderstandings and miscommunications. These problems are largely avoidable.

Avoid Travel Mistakes and Mix-Ups

- Do your due diligence. Invest extensive time in travel research. Explore *all* options.
- Get everything in writing. Read the fine print
- Don't make assumptions. Question anything you don't understand.
- Confirm and re-confirm all reservations.
- Develop a Plan B . . . and Plan C . . . just in case.
- Protect your travel investment. Charge travel on a major credit card and purchase travel insurance.
- Keep your cool. When misunderstandings or miscommunications occur, they are resolved more quickly with less stress when you have a reasonable and realistic attitude.

Let's take a look how to avoid or minimize the impact of some common travel snags and snafus.

Errors Booking Travel Online

What a deal! You've found an incredible airfare. Quick, click on it? No! Slow down and check it out again. When things go wrong with online booking, it's frequently human error. The hand is quicker than the eye and it gets you in trouble. Double and triple check the date, times and destination for the flight. Be sure the city you are booking is the right city. Paris, Texas is a long way from Paris, France. Check the date by looking at a calendar. Is May 16 a Saturday or is it a Sunday? Are you booking a 5 a.m. or a 5 p.m. flight? Are you looking at a different time zone? Learn air lingo. What restrictions apply to the flight? Is the ticket non-changeable and non-transferable? Is there telephone support for the booking site? If something goes awry or you have questions, can you talk to a human being?

After all the double checks, go one step further to avoid unpleasant surprises. Call the airline, the hotel, or the tour company. With the information on your screen or printed out in front of you, ask questions. Clarify terms. Confirm prices and restrictions. Ask if there are better prices or other options available. If you are satisfied with the answers and sure this deal is for you, click away. Use a major charge card for back-up. If you don't get what you paid for and you have a case against the provider, your credit card company may provide recourse.

Your Much-Awaited Cruise Cancels

The travel agent or cruise line just called and your cruise has been cancelled. Depending on your flexibility, this situation can work in your favor. We booked a cruise on Celebrity Cruises to Hawaii. A brand-new ship. We could hardly wait! Bad news came, about a month before the cruise. The ship was delayed in production and our cruise was cancelled. The good news: If we could travel a month later we would get another 50% off the great cruise price we already had. We delayed our travel for a month and enjoyed a wonderful cruise at a real bargain price.

If bad news comes, in the form of a cancellation, take a deep breath! Ask what the cruise line or tour company will do for you to make up for your disappointment and inconvenience? (While the company may not be obligated to do anything for you, good customer service calls for something more than just a returned deposit or cruise fare.) If the answer is "nothing," get your money back and take your business elsewhere.

Flight Delays

You arrive early at the airport to combat the check-in and security lines, only to find the word "DELAYED" next to your flight number. Proceed immediately to the ticket counter or the nearest airline representative. Find out what the delay is and when you will be on your way. If you encounter long lines at the ticket counter and can't locate a customer service representative pronto, grab your cell phone (don't travel without one). If you did your pre-flight homework, you have the telephone number for airline reservations. If you really did your homework, you know what other flight options are available and your rights as a traveler (See *Favorite Resources*). Ask what caused the delay. Knowing the cause of the delay determines your alternatives. If your flight is delayed, cancelled, or you miss a connection due to a "force majeure event" (Acts of God, bad weather, civil insurrection, war, hostilities, labor-related disputes, or shortage of labor or fuel), your alternatives and your rights are limited. The airline will probably try to re-route you, but they have no real obligation other than a refund. Ouch! That does not solve the immediate problem!

If the problem is weather or air traffic at your departure or your destination airport, you have to wait it out with everyone else. Find a seat, get a good book and settle in. Stay in the area. Keep your eyes and ears open for a hint of changes. Call reservations periodically to get the latest update. When you know connections are going to be missed, call reservations again. If the delay is at a city where you are making a connection (not your final destination) ask about being re-routed to avoid that connection.

If the delay is a result of a mechanical or crew scheduling problem, politely ask the agent to apply Rule 240. (The fact you know about Rule 240 usually gets some attention.) Rule 240 is a regulation requiring airline carriers to put you on the next flight out, even if is with a competitor or in business or first class, if necessary. It applies only to delays that are within the airline's control; not force majeure events. In addition to flight bookings, Rule 240 covers certain amenities such as hotel rooms, meals, and telephone calls. Check out **www.mytravelrights.com** for Rule 240 information for individual airlines.

Travel Experience: We had it all planned so well. We booked, six months in advance, a flight from Barcelona to Atlanta following a cruise. About two weeks before the cruise, I checked our flight itineraries on Delta's website. To our dismay, our great flight was "gone" and in its place was a terrible connection through New York JFK airport to Atlanta . . . not even on the same day as our original flight. A call to reservations initially provided no help. The agent informed us the travel agent must have changed the flight. Having done our homework, we already knew the Barcelona-to-Atlanta flight was cancelled on Delta's website. Next, the agent began to quote "rules" about not being able to accommodate us the day that we were originally booked because we were an "S" fare. At this point, Hank mentioned that the entire problem was caused by a cancellation by Delta and not a "force majeure." He added that it seemed Rule 240 should be applied. After a moment's silence, the agent said he would get a supervisor. Within three minutes, we were re-booked on a competitor airline on the same day and almost the same hour we were originally booked on Delta.

> **Travel Wisdom: Don't assume you can book early and forget it. Continue to check your reservation from time to time to avoid last-minute surprises. Number two: One would assume that good customer service would have prevailed and from the beginning. Not so. Do not depend on the airline to "do the right thing" without some nudging. Know your rights.**

> **Travel Wisdom Reminder: Never stand in a long line to get re-booked for a delay or especially a cancellation. Call the airline reservations number from your cell phone or a pay phone. Space is limited on alternative flights. Every minute counts!**

> **Travel Wisdom: Never pass up the chance to take an earlier flight. There are many opportunities for airline delays and cancellations. If you discover an earlier flight and can get it, take it . . . even if you have to spend more time in a connecting city. Important note: You can only take advantage of an earlier flight in a connecting city if you haven't checked a bag. Another good argument for carry-on bags.**

Overslept? Caught in Traffic? Missed Your Flight?

Get a back-up alarm clock. Allow ample time to travel to the airport. Get the picture? Don't miss your flight due to your own error! But, if something unavoidable happens and you do miss your scheduled flight, accept the fact that you have **no rights.** If you are not at the gate by the check-in deadline, the airline can and will cancel your seat.

Plead your case when you arrive at the airport. Throw yourself on the agent's mercy. Hopefully, the airline can book you on another flight. Expect to pay a hefty change fee. Don't be surprised if you have to "stand by" for an empty seat.

If the delay happens at home or enroute to the airport and you know you are going to miss your flight, call airline reservations and ask to be re-booked. The change fee will still apply, but you may be able to confirm a later flight.

Travel Wisdom: Remember to re-confirm your return flight if there is a change in your original ticketing; otherwise your return flight may be cancelled because you did not take your original flight and the computer assumes you won't be returning.

What Do You Mean There Are No More Seats?

You arrive at the gate and discover the flight is "a little **oversold.**" Saying a flight is a little oversold is like saying someone is a "little pregnant." What do you mean there are no seats? You have a confirmed reservation!

Overbooking occurs when the airline takes more flight reservations than there are seats on the aircraft. Airlines do this all the time . . . some more than others. They are betting on statistics that some passengers won't show up. Alas, everyone shows up. So, someone gets left behind . . . better known as "bumped." There is a vast difference in *voluntary* versus *involuntary* bumping

When you hear announcements at the gate asking for "volunteers," the flight is oversold and the airline is seeking volunteers to give up their seat. If you volunteer to be bumped, you are agreeing to give up your seat on this flight and take a later flight . . . in exchange for a "deal." It may or may not be to your advantage to answer the call and volunteer to be bumped. Once you volunteer and accept the deal, you are stuck with that deal.

Before you agree, know exactly what the deal is. For instance:

* Do you have an urgent reason to reach your destination at a certain time?
* Is the seat on the next flight guaranteed?
* When is the next flight?
* What if that flight is delayed or cancelled? What protection will you get?
* What happens to your checked bags?
* Is the airline offering a free ticket for a future flight or cash or both?
* What are the restrictions on the free ticket?
* If you have to stay overnight, will the airline pay for a hotel and meals in addition to the ticket?

Sometimes the deal is not a deal. Other times, especially when there are multiple oversold seats involved, the deal involves everything from a free ticket to monetary compensation. Sometimes there are enough volunteers. Other times, the initial offer gets sweetened because there are no volunteers. It is advantageous to the airline to get volunteers rather than bump passengers involuntarily.

> **Travel Wisdom: If you've done your homework, you can quickly decide whether it will benefit you to volunteer to be bumped. Know your rights. Know your alternatives. Move fast if you decide to accept the call!**

> **More Travel Wisdom: If you decide to get bumped in exchange for a free ticket, watch the expiration date. Over 50% of free tickets expire without being used.**

What if you get bumped involuntarily? There are very clear FAA and DOT guidelines to protect passengers denied boarding due to overbooking. Be sure the airline has asked for volunteers if you are about to be bumped. It also pays to know your compensation rights.

You may get no compensation if:
- Your reservation was not confirmed.
- You cancelled or changed your reservations along the way and did not re-confirm your return flight. (It happened to us!)
- You check in after the airline deadline.
- The airline gets you a seat on another flight that arrives within one hour of your originally scheduled flight.
- The aircraft has sixty seats or less. (Watch out for commuter flights. Oversells are frequent and the rules do not necessarily apply.)
- The flight is in-bound to the U.S. or totally outside the country.
- The flight is a charter. (Again, rules do not apply.)

If you are entitled to compensation, there are also guidelines that determine how much you may receive
- If the airline gets you a seat on another domestic flight that arrives over one hour but less than two hours after your scheduled flight, you are entitled to an amount equal to your fare for that portion of your travel (maximum $200.00).
- If the next seat is on a flight over two hours later, you are entitled to two times the amount of your fare for that portion of travel (maximum $400.00).
- In addition to compensation, you are entitled to keep your original ticket for use at a later date or request an "involuntary refund" for the unused portion of the ticket.

- You are also entitled to necessary hotel stays, meals, phone calls and other inconvenience perks. Approach with diplomacy, but sharpen your negotiation skills.

If you feel you are being treated unfairly, you have the right to decline any offers and sue. Think this over carefully. No matter how outraged you are. Be sure you are ready for the time, trouble, and possible expense involved in a lawsuit. Courts usually rule in favor of the airline if the required guidelines were met.

Don't think it's worth the hassle to get voluntarily or involuntarily bumped?
Take these steps to help avoid being bumped:
1. Learn which airlines consistently oversell flights and avoid them if possible. (**www.dot.gov/airconsumer/index1.htm**).
2. Be sure your flight is confirmed. If there is not an OK in the status box on your ticket, it is not confirmed.
3. Arrive early at the gate.
4. Fly non-stop.
5. Fly as early in the day as possible. If there's a problem, there are more options.
6 Avoid the last flight of the day—especially on Fridays.
7. Be sure you have a seat assignment. No assignment when a reservation is made is a good indication the flight is oversold and increases the odds of being bumped.
8. Board as soon as possible. If you delay, your seat could be "up for grabs."
9. Join the airline's frequent flyer program.

Overweight Baggage

Avoid overweight baggage by planning and preparation. Charges for overweight baggage are high. Pack smart. Weigh your bag at home while there is still time to lighten up. Split one bag into two bags rather than overstuffing and overweighting a single bag. It's to late to pare down once you are at the airport. Overweight? Pay up . . . grin and bear it. Learn your lesson only once.

Your Brand-New Bag Is Damaged by the Airline

Prevention is a key to avoiding damage. Don't over pack. Overstuffed bags strain seams and zippers. If you purchase a new piece of luggage, keep the receipt. Take a dated photograph of your luggage before and after you close the bag. (This photo is also helpful if your bag is lost.) Inspect your bags carefully at baggage claim. Report any damage *before* leaving the airport.

Where's My Bag?

There are two degrees of this problem. First, your bag does not arrive with you but shows up on a later flight and gets delivered to your door. Second, your bag never arrives. It disappears in the "Airline Baggage Black Hole."

There's also good news. Baggage tracking technology has improved dramatically.

According to the Department of Transportation (DOT), mishandled baggage claims average only about five for every one thousand passengers. Statistics also indicate that 97% of checked baggage arrives on the correct flight and only .005% of checked bags are lost forever. The odds are with you. The bad news: If your bag is delayed or lost you don't care about statistics! Wise travelers take precautions to prevent lost bags . . . or help the airline return them quickly.

- **Before you leave home, remove all old baggage tags.** Avoid having a scanner or baggage handler read the destination tag from your last trip and misroute your bag.

- **Place identification on the outside and inside of every piece of luggage.** Include a copy of your itinerary and hotel or cruise ship name and address on top of the items in your bag. This helps locate you while you are away from home.
- **While you are at it, put your name and address on other travel items such as laptops, cell phones, cameras and eyeglasses.** If these items are left behind, with no identification, there is little chance of a happy reunion.
- **Split your travel wardrobe and necessities between two bags.** If one bag goes astray, you'll still have half your things.
- **Keep a detailed packing inventory.** Take a copy with you in a carry-on and leave one at home. It's much easier to have a prepared inventory if there is a problem than to have to reproduce one from memory. (Bonus: It makes a great future packing checklist.)
- **Take all "must haves" with you in a carry-on bag.**
- **At check-in, make sure your bags are tagged correctly to your final destination, not a stop in-between.** Find the three-letter code for your destination ahead of time and be sure it is the one used.
- **Guard your baggage claim tags.** They are your only proof of checked baggage.
- **If your bags don't arrive with you, file a lost bag claim before leaving the airport—including a description of your bag and its contents.** If you have to surrender your claim tags, ask for a copy or a receipt for them. Leave a local telephone number for delivery and updates. Get a telephone number to check on your claim.

What can you expect from the airline if your bag is delayed or disappears forever? Be prepared to negotiate. If you are prepared, that means you have receipts, photos, and a detailed inventory to increase your odds of a fair settlement.

Travel Experience: Don't be too sure the airline can't lose your bag even if you don't fly! We drove to Tampa for a cruise. Had a great seven-day getaway, only to disembark and find we had no luggage to claim. Cruise representatives were not overly helpful, so we finally filed a claim with the cruise line and went home "bag less." A week went by; no word from the cruise line. One night we received a call from TWA in Kansas City. They informed us they were holding our bags and needed to know what flight we were on when they were misrouted. The agent had a difficult time believing we had not been on any flight with any airline. After we assured them that we were savvy travelers and knew when we did or did not travel by air, our bags were eventually shipped to our home airport for pick-up. Good thing we had identification on them or we would have never seen them again. This happened before 9/11. We shudder to think what might happen to "kidnapped" bags today.

The Lost Airline Ticket

Since electronic tickets have become the norm there are fewer lost ticket dilemmas. If you request and get a paper ticket, pick it up at the airport or travel agent's office to avoid a loss through the mail or the ticket not arriving in time for your flight. If you use a paper ticket, record the ticket number and all flight details in your travel information log. (Remember?) Notify the airline as soon as possible if your ticket is misplaced at home or enroute. Provide the ticket number to speed replacement.

Now . . . the bad news. There is almost always a replacement fee. You will have to pay for a new ticket and wait for a refund on the lost ticket. **Best advice: Don't lose that paper ticket!**

The Hotel from Hell

The lovely, spacious room pictured in the hotel brochure or on the website turns out to be a drab, dismal dump! Or . . . the room is beautiful, but there's no hot water, the air conditioning doesn't work, or an entire college fraternity is partying in the next room.

Wait . . . even if everything looks okay, feels okay and smells okay when you open the door. Don't undress, unpack, and settle in until you check out a few essentials. Test the door and window locks. Be sure the linens are fresh and clean. Does the toilet flush? Is there hot water? Is the bed comfortable? Look outside. Is there a truck depot or nightclub right outside your window that will disturb you? Is the beautiful advertised view actually a brick wall or parking garage?

If the room is not acceptable, return immediately to the front desk. Ask for another room, a refund, or a lower rate. If the front desk clerk is not responsive, ask for the manager.

Hopefully, you have copies of your confirmation and amenities promised. Be rational, reasonable, and specific about resolving the problem. Take notes or photos to document your claim if your complaint is not immediately resolved.

It also helps to join hotel frequent-stay programs. Almost all major hotel chains offer programs with rewards ranging from free stays to free breakfasts and other amenities. More important, frequent-stay status gives you more "clout" for problem resolution.

Lost or Stolen Credit Cards/Passport

Every traveler's nightmare. Savvy travelers plan ahead and protect their travel funds and critical travel documents.

- **Diversify your assets.** Always take more than one form of travel money. We take traveler's checks, an ATM card, two different credit cards, and some cash.
- **Don't carry it all in one place.** Divide cards and cash in two or more places. If traveling as a couple, take different credit cards. If something happens to one, you still have a valid charge card. Take one credit or ATM card and some of your cash when you shop. Lock the rest in the hotel safe. No safe? Hide cards and cash in unlikely places such as tampon boxes or vitamin bottles. Lock your passport in the room or master hotel safe. Do not take it shopping. Take one of the copies you made before you left home.
- **Lay all of your credit cards and forms of identification (driver's license, passport, insurance cards, etc.) out on a copy machine and make a one-page copy of them.** Write the emergency number for customer service above or below each card copy. Keep one copy in your luggage. Give one to a travel companion. Leave one at home.
- **In the event of credit card loss or theft, cancel the card/ cards immediately**. Be glad you made copies of the backs and fronts of the cards to facilitate cancellation. Also be glad you have your back-up travel funds. (See *Chapter Four—The Dollars and Sense of Travel.*)
- **If you lose your passport.** Contact the embassy or consulate office for passport replacement. Having a copy of the inside information page will expedite replacement. Also helps to have two spare passport photos tucked away with your travel documents.

In the Event of a Crisis, Natural Disaster, or Illness

The terrorist attack of September 11, 2001 had repercussions for travelers worldwide. People were stunned, scared, and stranded. There are obviously no guaranteed ways to avoid natural or manmade disasters. There is no way to ensure you will not become ill or have an accident. We don't want to discourage you from travel in any way, but we do want to help you protect your safety and wellbeing.

- **Know before you go**. Research safety-related conditions during your travel planning stage. Avoid travel to threatened areas and those with adverse health advisories.
- **Find the address and telephone number for the embassy or consulate office in all the countries you are visiting.** Include this information in your travel documents log. When you arrive, physically locate the embassy/consulate office. If you are on an extended stay, register with the office so that you can be contacted in the event of an emergency. If problems arise, don't hesitate to contact them immediately and follow their advice.
- **Do not cut travel expenses by skipping travel insurance.** There are many horror stories about uninsured travelers becoming ill or being involved in an accident far from home with no resources. (See *Chapter Four* for detailed travel insurance information.)
- **Take copies of critical medical records with your physician's name and telephone number.** This is especially important if you have a chronic condition or allergy that could become life threatening.
- **Record and carry names and contact numbers for at least three relatives or close friends.** Keep the numbers with you at all times. These numbers are your lifeline home if you are incapacitated.
- **If you participate in activities separate from travel companions, place a hotel business card in your pocket or wallet.** Without this card, emergency officials will have no way to locate your travel companions if something happens to you.
- **Keep a cell phone (or prepaid calling card) handy . . . at home and abroad.** Consider renting an international cell

phone for travel abroad. Always carry a prepaid calling card for emergency calls or just calls to say, "All is well."

- **Re-read *Chapter Five—Travel Health and Safety.*** Make sure you and your traveling companions are all familiar with **LACES.**

Fortunately, travel problems are an exception rather than the rule. When you encounter a problem, we hope it is a minor one and the tips we've provided will help you respond effectively rather than react with panic. In retrospect, minor problems often become entertaining travel stories or amusing memories. A final thought about travel problems: Expect the best and your expectations will almost always be met.

No pessimist ever discovered the secrets of the stars, or sailed to an   uncharted land, or opened a new heaven to the human spirit.

—— Helen Keller

CHAPTER EIGHTEEN

MAKING THE MEMORIES LAST

**Life is not measured by the number of breaths we take,
but by the number of moments that take our breath away.**
— *Unknown*

It's been a month since you came home. Your photos are stuffed in a shoebox in the closet. Your trip seems like a dream . . . the memories are fading. Try these tips to improve and capture your travel memories during travel, and preserve, enjoy, and share them for years to come.

Seek Out Memorable Travel Experiences

Of course, you want to visit the magnificent monuments, imposing palaces, historical landmarks, and hot tourist spots you've always read about. Part of travel education is immersing yourself in the history and flavor of the Coliseum in Rome, the Parthenon in Greece, the ruins of Pompeii, the beauty of the Eiffel Tower or Taj Mahal. While these places contribute to your memories, there are other small, subtle memory makers that will stay in your heart and mind long after the castles and cathedrals merge and become a blur.

Many travelers rush from tour to tour, madly snapping photos and video from windows of tour buses as scenery flashes by. When the film is developed and you are reviewing your photos at home, the cathedrals and castles all begin to look alike. Was this in Barcelona or Brussels? Berlin or Budapest? Not to mention the glare of the bus windows . . . and the backs of other traveler's heads! (More on better travel photos shortly.)

See the sights; then spend some time off the frantic tourist path. Relax at a sidewalk café, sip a glass of wine, and watch the world go by. Savor the sunset over the harbor or sunrise from the highest spot in town. Talk to children and old people. Both offer interesting perspectives on their world.

Travel Memory: When our sons were young (too young for this trip) we took them to the Grand Canyon. The most striking memory they both have was not the grandeur of the scenery, but of a little chipmunk that came up right at our feet while we were looking over the rim of the canyon. We caught a wonderful photo of their delight in this small unexpected pleasure.

We've discovered our best memories are the unexpected little events that occur during travel. Eat in a restaurant where locals eat. Order a regional dish you've never tasted. Consider staying at a local bed-and-breakfast—or with a local family—instead of at the American-style Holiday Inn. Hire a local guide for a walking tour and get "behind the scenes."

Travel Memory: One of our most enjoyable and memorable travel experiences was a walking tour of Chinatown in San Francisco with Shirley Torres-Fong. We visited a Chinese medicine shop where the doctor was seeing patients in the rear of the shop while the herbal prescriptions were mixed by two very elderly gentlemen from drawers with hundreds of herbs. We got a quick sneak peek at the activity in a mahjong parlor where the tiles were flying and conversation was brisk. We enjoyed green tea at a tearoom. We visited a grocery with exotic offerings from around the world. We witnessed the funeral of a wealthy Chinese citizen and a dragon parade with students. A *dimsum* lunch at one of Torres-Fong's favorite "off the beaten path" restaurants was incredible. All in all, the behind–the-scene sights, sounds, and smells created a wonderful memory!

Take new knowledge home with you. Attend a lecture at a local university or take a cooking or art appreciation class. Research the Internet during your planning stage for educational opportunities at your destination. You may even be able to "write off" some of the trip expenses if you can combine some education that applies to your business.

Travel Experience: On a recent cruise, we met a charming woman who writes cookbooks. She attends the cooking demonstrations, wine tastings, and galley tours and collects shipboard recipes. A great way to mix business and pleasure.

Keep a Travel Journal

I regret not keeping a travel journal beginning from my early days as a flight attendant. It would be so much fun now to look back and remember people, places, and events that have been lost in time.

Keep a small travel journal close at hand during your trip. Make it a point to write in it every day. Include stories about people you meet or observe. Write about funny (or not-so-funny) things that happen. Jot down facts or comments you want to remember. Write about your emotions: how you feel about what you are doing and seeing. Be sure to date each entry. Your travel journal could become a travel book!

> **Travel Journal Excerpt: March 2001. Ship docked in Maui this morning. For the past twenty-four hours we watched magnificent Orcas breaching all around the ship. It is thrilling to hear them blow as they surface. Was not aware before this trip, they migrate to Hawaii during this time of the year to bear their young. Met one of the most delightful women of my lifetime today. We were greeted at the dock with traditional hula dancers . . . and a not-so-traditional one! Miss Daisy calls herself the oldest Hula Girl in Hawaii. At ninety-one years young, she greeted disembarking passengers as if they were old friends. When we had our photo taken together, she looked at me and said, "Darling, don't say 'cheese.' Say 'sex,' it makes for a prettier smile." Her life story was fascinating. Wish I could have spent the entire day with her.**

Getting the Best Travel Images

Choose the right type of camera for your trip. Unless you are a skilled photographer, forget cameras with a multitude of settings. By the time you finally get the shot set up, the photographic moment may be lost. Although most serious photographers want a "good" camera, we find some of our best travel photos are from inexpensive disposable flash cameras (the 400 speed). These little cameras have come a long way in photo quality. If they are lost you may regret your lost photographs, but not a financial loss! Write your name and contact number on the camera cover. Digital (filmless) cameras also offer advantages such as the ability to take photos and delete unsatisfactory ones on-the-spot.

> **Travel Wisdom: When traveling with children over the age of five, give each of them their own one-use travel camera. After a little coaching on photographic techniques, you'll find their photographs will add to your travel memories.**

Create photographs that tell the story of your trip. Begin your photographic journey while you are packing, loading the luggage in the car or waiting in the airport lounge area. Rather than wildly snapping dozens of photos of those castles, cathedrals, and courtyards from a distance, take time to appreciate the beauty or grandeur of the scene. Then, look for photographic shots with an interesting perspective. For example, a castle reflected in the water or a beautiful bank of flowers in the foreground with the castle in the background. Look for amusing posters and signs and include them in your photos.

Watch for interesting people to include in your photos. Ask their permission to photograph them. It may cost a few coins or a dollar or so, but you'll get memorable photos. It's also important to get permission before snapping a picture due to privacy laws. You don't want your flash to spark an international incident while capturing a travel moment.

People make photographs more interesting and more memorable. Try to frame your shots so that they include your travel companions or other intriguing people. Offer to snap photos of fellow travelers or strangers with their cameras. Ask them to return the favor and snap you with your camera.

Don't waste your time or film trying to photograph people at a distance. When people are twenty feet away, their faces are a blur. Think foreground and background. Place people in the foreground (close) in your framed shot and buildings and scenery in the background (far). Likewise, don't attempt to take photographs at concerts or live shows. Besides the fact that constant flashes are extremely distracting to others in the audience, copyright laws usually prohibit flash photography and video. If you must have a shot of performers, purchase them. Finally, in case you lose or damage your film it always pays to supplement your photos and video with purchased postcards and beautiful photos of the landmarks and scenes that are important to your travel memories.

Preserving Your Travel Images

Once your film is developed, spend some time sorting your photographs. Throw away photos that are of poor quality. Select special photos for enlargements or copies for travel companions or friends. Purchase a good quality album and exercise your creativity. Fill it with your photos, postcards, and other mementos of your travels. Add captions and short stories from your journal. Share and enjoy your travel memories!

If I had my life to live over, I would take more trips. I would climb more mountains, swim more rivers and watch more sunsets.

— Nadine Stair

Appendix

Favorite Travel Resources

Travel resources number in the millions. As mentioned earlier, the sheer number of resources can be overwhelming and confusing. This chapter of *Travel Wisdom* shares our personal favorite travel websites, books, magazines and travel gear suppliers.

We hope you find the following resources helpful. As of publication date, all sources were current and accurate. We know how quickly resources change. Please accept our apologies if any resources are outdated. We're not affiliated with any of these resources. We get no compensation from suggesting them. And (of course) we accept no responsibility or liability for success or disappointment in utilizing any of the resources.

Travel Guidebooks

With all the assets the Internet has to offer, it's hard to beat a good, up-to-date guidebook from a reliable source. There are many good guidebooks on the market, but consider these questions to choose one for your trip:

- **Is the material in the guide current? Check the publication date.** Some publishers update their guides on a timely basis, others do not. Information in a guidebook that's several years old may no longer be accurate.

- **Can you take the guide along easily?** Will it fit easily in a backpack or tote bag? Leave the hardcover, beautifully bound tomes at home on the coffee table.
- **Does the guide contain the information you want and need?** Some guides devote more space to history and generic travel tips. Others are totally destination specific. Some give hotels and restaurants more space than attractions. Knowing your interests will help find the right format for your personal travel needs.

1. **Fodor's.** These guides deliver all-around destination information from A to Z. They are updated annually. Good travel size. Several different series, including language guides.
2. **DK Eyewitness Top 10 Travel Guides.** We love the Top Ten format and morning and evening activity sidebars. Lots of photographs and information bullets. Not as much depth as Fodor's, but more fun and "zippier." Hong Kong guide was right on target!
3. **Frommers.** Another of our favorite guide series. Loaded with great "finds" and "ratings." Easy to read and carry along.
4. **AAA Essential.** One of the smallest and most concise guidebook series on the market. Includes loads of sights, shopping, walks and tours with good AAA maps. We found the Essential Guide to Bali the best information available for that trip.
5. **Michelin in Your Pocket Travel Publications.** The smallest guides of all. Good maps on inside front and back covers. Information on accommodations and restaurants sketchy, but sightseeing fairly complete.
6. **Lonely Planet.** Good series. Geared more for independent travelers and adventure no-frills travel.

7. **Simple Guides To.** This series introduces travelers to the customs and etiquette of their destinations. Understanding customs and etiquette prevents embarrassment and helps you enjoy the culture of your destination.

Travel Magazines

I am a sucker for travel magazines. I love the articles, even the ones about destinations I have no interest in. I enjoy the advertising—a good way to get initial pricing overview. (Look at the people in the ads and get an idea of what age group a cruise line or tour is trying to attract.) Here are travel magazines we subscribe to on a regular basis:

1. **Travel & Leisure.** Offers a panorama of destinations and ideas. Publishes eight issues per year. Average subscription is $19.95.
2. **Budget Travel.** Published by Frommers. Primary focus: budget and low-cost travel destinations and ideas. Budget subscription rate of $12.00 for ten issues! A good value for the price and amount of information. Lots of tour and cruise advertising.
3. **Conde Nast Traveler.** More sophisticated and stylish than most travel publications. Another travel resource bargain at $12.00 for eight issues per year.
4. **National Geographic Traveler.** Lives up to other National Geographic standards, especially on destination articles. Priced at $14.95 for eight issues.
5. **Cruise Travel.** Loaded with the latest news from the cruise industry. Includes information on ships, ports, schedules and prices. Published six times a year for about $24.00. Caution: more advertising than articles. Review on newsstand before subscribing.
6. **travelgirl.** A great new savvy, sexy, and sophisticated travel magazine. (Not just for women!) Lots of tips and ideas. Published quarterly. Available on newsstands

Travel Gear

Although we purchase most of our travel gear from discount department stores like Wal-Mart or Target, from time to time, we find unique and indispensable travel gear from these sources.

1. **L. L Bean.** (800-221-4221). Has a separate travel gear catalog. Can't beat their silk long johns! (**www.llbean.com/ traveler**)
2. **Magellan's.** (800-962-4943) Wide range of travel necessities from travel wear to travel gadgets. Love their silk sarong. (**www.magellans.com**)
3. **TravelSmith.** (800-950-1600) Great selection of mix-and-match travel wear in latest wrinkle-free fabrics. Tencel jeans, for women and men, are a travel must. (**www.travelsmith.com**)
4. **Christine Columbus.** (800-280-4775) Travel needs for women and loads of travel tips! Great free packing checklist. (**www.christinecolumbus.com**)

Travel Wisdom: Before adding personal information to any website, especially credit card numbers, be sure you are on a secure website. The URL bar line at the top of the screen where the website name is changes from http:// to https:// when a site is secure. A pop-up box should also notify you a website is secure.

Travel Websites

Frequently we see a website listed only to find it no longer exists or has changed. We checked each of these websites and hope you'll still find them current and reliable:

General Travel Information Websites
1. **www.alltheweb.com** Largest index of Web pages in the world.
2. **www.worldtravelers.org** worldwide travel news and advisories.
3. **www.artoftravel.com** Tips and humor from independent travelers
4. **www.travelnotes.org** Detailed country backgrounds and travel articles.
5. **www.concierge.com** Upscale travel ideas and tips
6. **www.dotheresearch.com** Great site loaded with wide range of travel information from A to Z.
7. **www.savvytraveler.com** Latest travel trends, news and articles
8. **www.mytripandmore.com** Create your own travel plan
9. **www.towd.com** Non-commercial site. Has "worlds" of information about U.S. and international destinations. No advertising.
10. **www.justtravellinks.com** 300,000 links to travel guides and vacations. Arranged alphabetically.
11. **www.timeout.com** Online travel magazine
12. **www.frommers.com** Great site. Loaded with comprehensive travel information. Download your personalized mini-guides.
13. **www.fodors.com** Same as above. A good all-in-one site for all types of travel and destination info.
14. **www.travelnow.com** Explore travel packages and pricing.
15. **www.consumerworld.org/pages/travel.htm** Hundreds of links to travel resources.
16. **www.johnnyjet.cdom** Lots of "fun" travel info and links. Good free newsletter.
17. **www.1000traveltips.org** Truly thousands of travel tips from real travelers.
18. **www.freetraveltips.com** Good format and easy to use for travel tips.

19. **www.traveling-tips.com** Concise destination guides.
20. **www.travelchannel.com** What's scheduled on the Travel Channel and more.
21. **www.freetodo.net** Internet guide to free things to see and do in Europe and the U.S.
22. **www.igougo.com** A community of real travelers sharing their experiences. Over 100,000 photos!
23. **www.classictravelusa.com** Travel do's and don'ts. Packing lists. Excellent article on in-flight exercises.

Travel Websites for Women
1. **www.gutsywomentravel.com** Tips and trips of women only. Good, fun site!
2. **www.women-traveling.com** Tours and tips. 80% single travelers.
3. **www.christinecolumbus.com** Travel clothes, gear and great tips.
4. **www.voyage.gc.ca** Download a free 24-page book on travel for **women,** *On Her Way.*

Websites for Disabled Travelers
1. **www.access-able.com** Information on accessible destinations, cruise ships, air travel. Travel gear for disabled travelers.
2. **www.sath.org** Promotes awareness and respect for disabled travelers.
3. **www.dot.gov** Know your travel rights.
4. **www.accessiblejourneys.com** Company specializes in wheelchair group travel.

Travel with Children
1. **www.kidtravels.com** Personal stories and advice for travel with kids.
2. **www.about-family-travel.com** Promotes family travel. Good tips column.

3. **www.momsminivan.com** Road travel with kids.
4. **www.travelforkids.com** Worldwide info on things to see and do with children.
5. **www.travelwithkids.com** Series of links to articles and ideas.
6. **www.havechildrenwilltravel.com** Excellent newsletter on travel ideas and info for families of all ages. Subscription with fee required.

Business Travel

1. **www.businesstravel.about.com** Compilation of business travel articles and resources.
2. **www.businesstrip.com** Loads of good info on all aspects of business travel.
3. **www.oag.com** Fee based. Online airline schedules. Great for Plan B.
4. **www.webflyer.com** Manage frequent miles and programs. Find out the latest in bonus promos.

Senior Travel

1. **www.travel.state.gov/olderamericans.html** The latest government facts, tips and warnings for senior travelers.
2. **www.seniorworld.com** Good resource for seniors for travel and more.
3. **www.smarterliving.com/senior** Overall good site for senior travel and day–to–day smart living.
4. **www.seniors-site.com/travel** Extensive info and checklists for mature travelers.
5. **www.aboutseniors.com.au./travel** More senior info
6. **www.aarp.com** Lives up to AARP standards. Reliable information and links.
7. **www.elderhostel.com** Great learning adventures for age 55 up.
8. **www.eldertreks.com** Adventure and nature travel for seniors.

Government Travel Information
1. **www.tsa.dot.gov** Current news and tips on clearing security.
2. **www.travel.state.gov** Latest travel warnings. You can also listen to warnings 24 hours a day at (202) 647-5225.
3. **www.americanpassport.com** Everything you need to know to get and keep a passport.
4. **www.customs.ustreas.gov** The facts and lots of them on what can and cannot come into and go out of the United States. Be sure to read carefully before international travel.
5. **www.dot.gov/airconsumer** Air consumer reports, records, and customer service plans.
6. **www.faa.gov** Easy-to-use site with lots of information on aviation safety and security. Includes on-time records and individual airline safety records.
7. **www.cdc.gov/travel** Health information on destinations. What you need to know before you go.
8. **www.who.int** International health reports.
9. **www.tsa.gov** Latest information about airport security.
10. **www.tsatraveltips.us** Great travel tips right from the security source.
11. **www.cia.gov** Worldwide information demographics of any country.

Cruise Travel
1. **www.cruisemates.com** Cruising from A to Z. One of our three favorite cruise sites!
2. **www.cruisecritic.com** Reviews from passengers on ships and cruise lines.
3. **www.cruisereviews.com** More reviews
4. **www.porthole.com** *Porthole* magazine website.
5. **www.e-cruiseworld.com** Latest cruise/ship news.
6. **www.cruise2.com** Largest non-profit site on the Internet. Everything from matching passengers with ship to sample menus. Another of our favorites!

7. **www.princesscruises.com** Princess Cruises. Check specials!
8. **www.celebrity-cruises.com** Celebrity Cruises.
9. **www.carnival.com** Carnival Cruises.
10. **www.costacruises.com** Costa Cruises.
11. **www.crystalcruises.com** Crystal Cruises. Check specials!
12. **www.disneycruise.com** Disney Cruises. Most family-oriented!
13. **www.hollandamerica.com** Holland American Cruises.
14. **www.rccl.com** Royal Caribbean Cruise Line.
15. **www.ncl.com** Norwegian Cruise Line.
16. **www.rssc.com** Radisson Seven Seas Cruises. Very upscale.
17. **www.seabourn.com** Seabourn Cruises. Upscale.
18. **www.silversea.com** Silversea Cruises. Upscale.
19. **www.windstarcruises.com** Windstar Cruises.
20. **www.uniworld.com** River barge cruises
21. **www.cruisehawaii.com** Like the name says!
22. **www.cruisewest.com** Small ship cruises in Alaska, California Wine Country, Baja, and more.
23. **www.deltaqueen.com** Steamboat cruising.
24. **www.riverbarge.com** River barge cruising.
25. **www.eurocruises.com** Cruises in Europe.

Flight Resources
1. **www.airlineandairportlinks.com** Incredible amount of information about every airline and virtually every airport. Print off airport diagrams for easy connections.
2. **www.mytripandmore.com** Great site. Links to all major airline, hotel, car rental, cruise line web sites and telephone numbers. Links to government travel-related websites. Click on currency and print a currency conversion cheatsheet.
3. **www.seatguru.com** Terrific website with seating diagrams on most major airlines, includes tips on legroom and which seats to avoid.

4. **www.webflyer.com** Compares frequent flyer programs and provides latest news in airline bonus offers.
5. **www.onetravel.com** Good comparison site.
6. **www.mytravelrights.com** Consumer rights center. Print out Rule 240 for your airline.
7. **www.extratv.warnerbros.com** Great site for Rule 240. Enter Rule 240 in search block. Print out a wallet-sized general version or click on individual airlines for their full version. Print and carry!
8. **www.johnnyjet.com** "Fun" site for general air travel. Good free newsletter.
9. **www.bestfares.com** Good for fare comparisons. Excellent travel tips.
10. **www.priceline.com** Auction site/read cautions! Good for comparisons.
11. **www.orbitz.com** Discount site for major airlines
12. **www.expedia.com** All **types of discount online bookings.**
13. **www.delta.com** Delta Air Lines.
14. **www.airtran.com** Air Tran Air Lines
15. **www.aa.com** American Air Lines
16. **www.continental.com** Continental Air Lines
17. **www.jetblue.com** Jet Blue Air Lines
18. **www.nwa.com** Northwest Air Lines
19. **www.iflyswa.com** Southwest **Air Lines**
20. **www.ual.com** United Air Lines
21. **www.usairways.com** US Airways
22. **www.frequentflyer.com** Find out all about frequent flyer programs.
23. **www.lastminutetravel.com** Check out last-minute deals on air travel, events, hotels, and more.

Train Travel
1. **www.trainweb.com** General info on rail travel.
2. **www.therail.com** More of the same.

3. **www.raileurope.com** Train travel in Europe . . . the in's and the out's.

4. **www.amtrak.com** Amtrak Site. Lots of good info.

5. **www.viarail.com** Canada's version on Amtrak. All about train travel in Canada.

6. **www.eurorail.com** Train travel in Europe, including rail passes.

Dining Out

1. **www.zagat.com** Now charging a membership fee. Offers some free info. Probably worth the fee for business travelers.

2. **www.fodors.com** Click on restaurant guide for your destination and sort by name, type of food and price.

3. **www.dine.com** Restaurant reviews for 175,000 locations. Must join but free.

4. **www.411dining.com** Major city dining guides and discount coupons.

5. **www.globaldining.com** Worldwide dining guides. Again, must join, but free.

6. **www.restaurants.com** Discount dining certificates for restaurants.

7. **www.dirona.com** A listing of distinguished restaurants of North America. Find award-winning restaurants in virtually any city.

Hotels

1. **www.1800usahotels.com** Database of U.S. hotels, bed -and-breakfast resource.

2. **www.bedandbreakfast.com** Great bed-and-breakfast resource.

3. **www.igww.com** Search huge database by type of lodging and destination. Everything from cabins to castles.

Tour Operators

1. **www.ustoa.com** Site for U.S. Tour Operators Association. Loaded with great information about independent/group tours. Order Smart Traveler's Planning Kit online or at 800-468-7862.
2. **www.tourvacationstogo.com** Good research site with many links to tour operators.
3. **www.travelhub.com** Doorway to travel agencies and tour packages. Good idea site.
4. **www.delta.com/vacations** Check out Delta Air Lines vacation packages.
5. **www.americanexpress.com** American Express vacation deals.
6. **www.saga.com** Saga Tours.
7. **www.tauck.com** Tauck Tours.
8. **www.collette.com** Collette Tours.
9. **www.grandcircle.com** Grand Circle Tours.
10. **www.insight.com** Insight Tours.
11. **www.aaa.com** Triple A Tours.

*Note: It's interesting and educational to compare offerings of listed tour groups.

Travel Insurance

1. **www.insuremytrip.com** Good site for comparing travel insurance from multiple companies.
2. **www.accessamerica.com** Compare insurance plans.
3. **www.travelex-insurance.com** More insurance quotes.
4. **www.travelguard.com**
5. **www.csatravelprotection.com** One of oldest and largest travel insurers.
6. **www.tripassured.com** No age penalty.
7. **www.medjet.com.** Air evacuation insurance for reasonable annual fee. Good resource for frequent travelers

Miscellaneous Web Resources

1. **www.unclaimedbaggage.com** Alabama warehouse that sells clothing, luggage, and merchandise officially declared "unclaimed" by the airlines.

2. **www.oanda.com** Click on currency conversion cheatsheet and print a pocket-sized guide to converting foreign currency. Great shopping resource!

3. **www.travlang.com** Learn important words, such as THANK YOU and PLEASE, in the language of your destination. Make a cheatsheet of key phrases. Even if you don't pronounce them exactly right, the effort will be appreciated.

4. **www.citypass.net** Purchase a CityPass for multiple attractions in popular American city destinations at significant discounts.

5. **www.mapblast.com** Free maps and directions.

6. **www.mapquest.com** More maps.

7. **www.mapsonus.com** And more maps.

8. **www.onlineweather.com** Worldwide weather.

9. **www.weather.com** More weather.

10. **www.traveletiquette.com.** Travel etiquette and culture guides for most countries.

Miscellaneous Travel Resources

When Things Go Wrong . . . Know Your Rule 240

Rule 240 was a requirement of the United States Federal Government before airline deregulation in 1978. Today, major airlines have filed "Conditions of Carriage" with the Department of Transportation (DOT). These Conditions of Carriage still guarantee their respective Rule 240s. In summary, Rule 240 states that an airline must deliver you to your destination within two hours of the originally scheduled flight time if (a) your flight is delayed or cancelled or (b) you miss your connection due to a delay that is the airline's direct fault. It does not apply to delays caused by "Acts of God" (force majeure events).

Each airline has its own Rule 240. Copies of Rule 240 are supposed to be kept at the ticket counter. Don't count on it. Print and carry a copy of Rule 240 for the airline you are flying with. Rule 240 for individual airlines can be found at **www.mytravelrights.com**, and at **www.airtravel.about.com** enter the search word Rule 240 and click on any link to individual airline listings. Often just the mention of "Rule 240" in a polite, but firm, manner will help you win this airline battle.

Appendix

TRAVEL WISDOM To-Do CHECKLISTS

Things To Do Three To Six Months Before Departure

1. Get serious about your research. Narrow down your choices. Book your trip.
2. Apply for passport/visas. Check the expiration date of current passport. Be certain it will not expire within six months during your trip.
3. Purchase travel insurance. Remember pre-existing conditions usually require certificate purchase within seven to ten days of trip purchase.
4. Take inventory of luggage and travel wear. Do you have everything you need? Are items in good repair?
5. Order new travel clothing or accessories.
6. Update personal information on credit cards, ATM cards, and driver's license. It's critical that all information be correct and consistent. Check expiration date on credit cards and driver's license.
7. Begin exercising to get in shape for travel demands.
8. Look into options for house sitters, pet boarding/ sitting, and any care needed for dependents left at home.
9. Set up as many payments as possible on automatic draft.
10. Keep your *Travel Resource Files* updated.

Add your own To-Do Items

Things to Do 30 Days Before Departure

1. Schedule a medical check-up. Get necessary vaccinations. Ask your physician about a Hepatitis A vaccination.
2. Make a dental appointment.
3. If you are driving, take your vehicle in for a complete road-safety check-up.
4. Validate and try out new ATM cards or credit cards to be sure they work as needed.
6. Check with your bank for daily limits on ATM withdrawals. Increase limit if needed.
7. Notify credit card companies that you are traveling out of area. Provide lists of destinations where cards may be used.
8. Confirm arrangements for house, pet or dependent care.
9. Develop instructions for house sitter or neighbor watching house. Include instructions for watering plants, alarm procedures in case of activation, mail pick-up, and emergency repairs. Make a list of contact numbers for your plumber, electrician, pool service, air conditioning/heating and lawn care providers.

Add your own To-Do Items

Things to Do One Week Before Departure

1. **Get luggage out.** Assemble clothes and necessities for packing. Begin packing.
2. **Make a test run** to the airport to gauge traffic, parking, check-in and security clearance times.
3. **Make four or five copies** (back and front) of all credit cards, ATM card, driver's license and information page of passport. Get two extra passport photos.
4. **Re-fill prescriptions.** Get copies of any medical records you might require in an emergency.
5. **Purchase back-up pair of eyeglasses or contacts.**
6. **Purchase a telephone calling card.** Learn to use it. Be sure it works.
7. **Check camera and purchase film.** Remember, do not pack film in luggage to be checked.
8. **Purchase automatic timers for lights and radio.**
9. **Take necessary items to dry cleaners.** Laundry other travel clothes.
10. **Avoid buying grocery items** that will spoil while you are away.
11. **Take valuables to safe deposit box.**
12. **Get traveler's checks from bank.** Order foreign currency if you must. (Review Dollars & Sense for travel fund recommendations.
13. **Break in new shoes** you will be wearing on trip!
14. **Place a hold on mail and newspapers delivery.**
15. **Make arrangements for lawn care.**

Add your own To-Do Items

Things To Do 48 Hours Before Departure

1. Reconfirm all reservations.
2. Get cash from bank.
3. Notify police and alarm company that you will be traveling. Leave emergency contact for person responsible for your home.
4. Give copies of itinerary to family and close friends. Be sure to place copy in carry-on and pack a copy inside checked bags.
5. Give copy of credit cards, ATM card, and passport to family member or trusted friend.
6. Do last-minute laundry.
7. Finish packing except last-minute items for carry-on.
8. Practice handling your bags. Loading them in the car. Carrying them around.
9. Be sure identification tags are on all bags—inside and outside—including carry-ons.
10. Set and test automatic timers on lights and radio.
11. Make a weather check to be prepared for changes.
12. Review packing lists.
13. Double check that all travel documents, tickets, etc., are complete and in your carry-on bag.
14. Purchase travel eats and treats.

Add your own To-Do Items

Things to Do the Day Before Departure

1. Clean out refrigerator. Empty all trash.
2. Wash dirty dishes.
3. Relocate houseplants to take advantage of rain and avoid direct sunlight. (I hook a garden hose with an oscillating sprinkler to our timed sprinkler system and group plants so that they get watered automatically each day when lawn system comes on.)
4. Fill car with gas and do final check of tire pressure and fluids if driving.
5. Check locks on all windows and doors.
6. Unplug electronics and appliances you will not be using.
7. Finish packing. Re-check packing list.
8. Get a good night's sleep.
9. Check your alarm clock for right setting. Set a back-up alarm.

Add your own To-Do Items

Things To Do the Day of Departure

1. Check that stove, oven and coffee pot are turned off.
2. Set air conditioner/heater, refrigerator, and water heater to desired setting.
3. Take out last-minute trash.
4. Double and triple check that all documentation is in hand.
5. Leave blinds and drapes in normal position.
6. Check all doors and windows are locked.
7. Check timers set.
8. Load bags in car.

Add your own To-Do Items

ENJOY YOUR TRIP!

TRAVEL WISDOM SAMPLE PACKING LISTS

Sample Packing List for Women
(10-Day or Longer Trip)

3 Pants, three-color scheme (i.e., red, black and grey or blue, grey and cream)
3 Skirts, same color scheme (mix prints and solids)
2 Jackets/cardigans (solids work best)
6 Shells/blouses (mix prints solids in three-color scheme)
3 Dresses (one "little black dress" for versatility)
1 Sarong (black works great; multitude of uses)
2 Swimsuits (never have to put on a wet suit)
2 Shorts (if tropical climate, such as a cruise or resort-- not appropriate wear in Asia or Europe)
1 pair of Tencel jeans
2 T-shirts (great to purchase along the way)
Nightgown and lightweight robe (use sarong as robe!)
Undies (5 pair panties, two bras, 2 pair trouser socks)
Only 3 pair of shoes including the ones you wear! (one pair dressy pumps, one pair walking, one pair sandals)
Shawl or evening wrap
Unique, inexpensive jewelry (8–10 pieces; one splashy piece for black dress at night) Several scarves/belts
Packable hat for bad weather/bad hair days
If traveling in cold climate, substitute or add these items
Silk or microfiber long johns (Land's End makes a great black silk set; can double as pajamas)
Warm wool hat and gloves
2 Jogging-type suits (or lightweight sweats/sweaters; think layers)
Gore-Tex jacket (windproof, waterproof, and incredibly warm!)

Sample Packing List For Men. 10-day or longer trip

3 pair pants (black, navy, khaki or grey)
1 Sports coat or blazer
On business or more formal trips add one suit, three dress shirts and ties
6 Casual shirts, lightweight crew-neck sweaters, or golf shirts; keep to colors in pants)
1 pair Tencel jeans
3 T-shirts (buy more along the way!)
2 shorts (if tropical, same rules apply for appropriate wear)
2 Swimsuits
Sleepwear
Underwear (4 briefs, two undershirts, 3 or 4 socks)
2 pair shoes (3 counting the ones you wear)

In cold climates, add the following:
Gore-Tex jacket
Wool hat and gloves.
Long johns (Land's End black silk—warm and comfortable, can substitute for pajamas)
2 Jogging suits or lightweight sweats
2 Sweaters

Sample Travel Necessities Checklists

The following checklist may seem like a lot of "stuff." Most take very little room and greatly increase your travel comfort and pleasure.

Important items for carry-on
Travel tickets and confirmations
Passport/visas (extra copy separately in case of loss)
Health/vaccination certification/records
Travel insurance certificate/emergency contact number
Photo identification (in addition to passport)
Frequent flyer card
Medical insurance card
Credit cards/ATM card (extra copies of all cards separately in case of loss)
Cash (include $20.00 in crisp one-dollar bills)
Detailed travel itinerary (extra copy in top of checked bags; travel information, notebook and pen)
Contact numbers for family/friends
Currency exchange and language cheatsheets
Reading material
Note: A good document holder helps in keeping the aforementioned items together and organized
One change of clothes
Prescription medicines, over-the-counter meds taken regularly, eyeglasses/contacts
Folding umbrella/poncho
Camera and film
Bottle of water and gourmet snacks
Inflatable neck pillow and lightweight blanket or wrap
Toiletries for one or two nights
Flashlight

Additional Necessities and Accessories:

Hat or visor
Pair of small binoculars (Carlson makes good ones)
Antibacterial hand gel (use often)
Hepa-masks (precautionary in case of flu outbreak)
Wet wipes (trust on this one—better than toilet paper)
Fabric softener sheets (many uses)
Playing cards (good as small gifts along the way)
"Throw away" wallet
Sewing kit/safety pins
Duct tape (not the whole roll; wind some around a pen)
Wrinkle-free spray
Door stopper (extra security)
Several Ziploc bags (a million uses!)
Pre-paid telephone calling card
Ear plugs/eye shade
A black garbage bag
Collapsible tote bag/backpack for day trips and overflow souvenirs
Alarm clock (Remove battery during flight to avoid accidental alarm activation. Take extra batteries.)
Voltage converter (I nearly set fire to my hair in Singapore trying to do without one; dumb move)

Personal Health and Hygiene Necessities Checklist

Prescriptions (in carry-on bag; leave in original bottles/take copies)
Pain reliever
Cold/sinus tablets
Imodium
Alka-Seltzer/Tums or other anti-acids
Laxative
Anti-nausea (Bonine, Dramamine, herbal ginger)
Antibiotic cream such as Neosporin
Zinc oxide
Insect repellant (if tropical travel)
Sunscreen and sunglasses
Melatonin (great for jet lag and time changes)
Moleskin (keep blisters away when walking a lot)
Fever strip
Eye drops
Contact lens/eyeglasses, copy of prescriptions
Case for contacts
Razor or shaver/shaving cream
Hairspray/hair gel
Tube of bath gel (hate those tiny hotel soaps!)
Tampons/panty liners
Birth control
Shampoo (does double duty as laundry soap)
Toothpaste/toothbrush/dental floss
Comb/brush/curling iron
Hairdryer (check ahead . . . may be supplied by hotel/ship)

IMPORTANT INTANGIBLE TRAVEL CHECKLIST

Appetite for Adventure
Bundle of Boldness
Cache of Curiosity, Creativity, and Cheerfulness
Dash of Delight and Daring
Element of Enthusiasm
Focus on FUN
Gift of Generosity
Hoard of Humor
Incredible Imagination
Jacket of Joy
Kettle of Kindness
Love of Life
Magic of Making the Most of MOMENTS
Nerve to Negotiate
Order of an Open Mind . . . and Optimism
Pack of Patience
Quest for the Quixotic
Reserve of Respect
Slice of Spontaneity
Ton of Thankfulness . . . and Thoughtfulness
Unlimited Understanding
Verve, Vim and Vigor
Wealth of Wisdom . . . Travel Wisdom!
Xanadu of (e)Xcitement (This was a tough one!)
Zest and Zeal

Appendix

AND THESE ARE A FEW OF OUR FAVORITE THINGS

Top Ten Travel Adventures (So Far)

1. 90-minute F-16 fighter jet ride (Lynne)
2. Hot-air balloon ride in California and Sonoran Desert
3. Helicopter ride over the crater of Kilauea Volcano.
4. The Grand Bazaar in Istanbul, Turkey.
5. Swimming with the giant manta rays at Grand Cayman Island.
6. Seeing the Monkey Dance at sundown in Bali
7. Chinese New Year in Hong Kong
8. Aerial tram through the canopy of the rain forest in Costa Rica
9. Whale watching in Alaska and Maui
10. Every cruise

Top Ten Still-to-Do Adventures

1. Cruise around the world.
2. Walk the Great Wall of China.
3. Dive on the Great Barrier Reef in Australia.
4. See the pyramids along the Nile.
5. Take a river barge trip through France.

6. Attend culinary classes in Tuscany.
7. Take a train trip on the Orient Express.
8. Dive on a WWII shipwreck in the Pacific (Hank)
9. Fly in a glider and a blimp.
10. Be contestants on "The Amazing Race."

Top Ten Favorite Cities in the United States

1. Fort Walton Beach/Destin, Florida
2. San Francisco, California
3. New York City, New York
4. Washington, D.C.
5. New Orleans, Louisiana
6. Mendocino, California
7. San Diego, California
8. Seattle, Washington
9. Boston, Massachusetts
10. Key West, Florida

Top Ten Favorite International Cities

1. Hong Kong
2. Paris
3. Rome
4. Istanbul
5. Venice
6. Barcelona
7. Reykjavik
8. London
9. Vancouver
10. Cannes

Top Ten Favorite Hotels

1. The Chedi in Ubud, Bali
2. Little River Inn, Mendocino, California
3. Atlantis Resort, Nassau
4. Ocean Reef Resort, Florida Keys
5. Princess Hotel, Acapulco

6. Peninsula Hotel, Hong Kong
7. Ritz Carlton, New Orleans
8. Topaz Hotel, Washington, D.C.
9. Marriott Marquis, Times Square, New York City (for location primarily)
10. Princess Hotel, Scottsdale, Arizona

Top Ten Favorite Dining Experiences

1. Felix's – Peninsula Hotel – Hong Kong
2. The Stinking Rose – San Francisco
3. Café Sport – San Francisco
4. Picnicking on the grounds of V. Sattui Winery in Napa
5. Sidewalk cafes on La Rambla in Barcelona, Spain
6. Beignets and Café au Lait, Café du Monde, New Orleans
7. Beachwalk Café, Destin, Florida
8. Two Quail – Washington, D.C.
9. Theme lunches on any Crystal Cruise
10. Seafood Buffet, Ocean Reef Resort, Florida Keys

Favorite Airport in the World
Changi International Airport, Singapore

Favorite Airline
Singapore Airlines

We'd love to hear from you. Please share your favorites with us at travelwisdom@cox.net

Indexing

Printed in the United States
1481200004B/1-54